ADVANCE PRAISE FOR

MAJORING
in CHANGE

"In *Majoring in Change*, Allison Butler has produced an important and timely book for anyone concerned about education and the real life impacts of the economic crisis. Using cutting-edge qualitative research, Butler skillfully captures the voices of those whom the American school system has failed. Her words bring to life the real victims and survivors whose schooling and futures have been shaped by neoliberal educational policies and a failing economy. Grounded in theoretically rich discussions, Butler offers a truly interdisciplinary perspective and boldly proposes media literacy as a foundation for the critical inquiry, technical skill, and fundamentals required for success in the twenty-first century."

—*Emilie Zaslow, Associate Professor, Communication Studies, Pace University*

MAJORING
in CHANGE

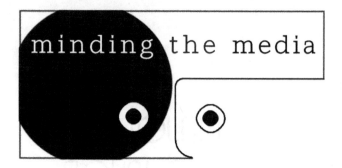

minding the media

CRITICAL ISSUES FOR LEARNING AND TEACHING

Shirley R. Steinberg and Pepi Leistyna
General Editors

Vol. 8

The Minding the Media series is part of both
the Peter Lang Education list and the Media and Communication list.
Every volume is peer reviewed and meets
the highest quality standards for content and production.

PETER LANG
New York • Washington, D.C./Baltimore • Bern
Frankfurt • Berlin • Brussels • Vienna • Oxford

ALLISON BUTLER

MAJORING
in CHANGE

Young People Use Social
Networking to Reflect on
High School, College and Work

PETER LANG
New York • Washington, D.C./Baltimore • Bern
Frankfurt • Berlin • Brussels • Vienna • Oxford

Library of Congress Cataloging-in-Publication Data

Butler, Allison.
Majoring in change: young people use social networking
to reflect on high school, college, and work / Allison Butler.
p. cm. — (Minding the media: critical issues for learning and teaching; v. 8)
Includes bibliographical references and index.
1. High school students—United States—Attitudes.
2. College students—United States—Attitudes.
3. Youth—United States—Attitudes.
4. High school students—United States—Social networks.
5. College students—United States—Social networks.
6. Youth—United States—Social networks.
7. Facebook (Electronic resource) I. Title.
LA229.B795   373.18—dc23   2011037651
ISBN 978-1-4331-1536-3 (hardcover)
ISBN 978-1-4331-1535-6 (paperback)
ISBN 978-1-4539-0240-0 (e-book)
ISSN 2151-2949

Bibliographic information published by **Die Deutsche Nationalbibliothek**.
Die Deutsche Nationalbibliothek lists this publication in the "Deutsche
Nationalbibliografie"; detailed bibliographic data is available
on the Internet at http://dnb.d-nb.de/.

Cover art by Ivan Forde

© 2012 Peter Lang Publishing, Inc., New York
29 Broadway, 18th floor, New York, NY 10006
www.peterlang.com

For sweet Charlotte Jane and ATB²
(who showed up early, but just a little too late for the last one)
Two embodiments of love & joy

And, always, for Mom, without whom I would be lost

CONTENTS

ACKNOWLEDGMENTS

This text is about a time of pivotal transition in young people's lives. It should come as no surprise that it was conceived and written in a time of pivotal transition in my own life. I have more people to thank than I would have thought possible at the outset of this project. Without them and their various, rich roles in my life, my own process of transition would have been less vibrant.

First, foremost and always, I thank my participants. Witnessing their development from just-barely-teenagers to young adults has been a truly awe-inspiring experience. After completing my first project with them, I could not let them go–I am regularly amazed by their strength in the face of great struggle, their courage, their heartfelt willingness to take risks and their emotional honesty.

Amazing friends and colleagues have proven invaluable to the whole process. Before leaving NYC, Jorja and Laura reminded me of bravery. Since living in Massachusetts, Anna, J, Amy, and Shannah take on that task on a regular basis. Thank you to Peter, who always keeps a watchful eye, and to Richard, who always keeps the doors open. Chyng Sun, thank you for always believing in me and connecting me with stupendous people in Massachusetts. When I first moved here, Fanny Rothschild and Michael Morgan took me in, showed me around and have become great friends. Wendy Nelson of Asnuntuck Community College, thank you for being such a staunch supporter and good friend. To my research assistant Nicholas Armata, thank you for knowing so much more about Facebook than I ever could. Thank you Lisa Henderson and Erica Scharrer of the University of Massachusetts, Amherst for bringing me onto the faculty. Thank you to the UMass students of Children, Teens & Media and Media & Education courses who tolerated my babbling on and on about the ideas in this research. Exponential thanks to Wendy Chen, who is *still* there for me and is *still* willing to read my drafts. I am blessed to work with a whole new group of talented young people; thank you Sahar, Uma, Oli, Rose, Jake and Hattie for making Friday mornings so thought provoking (and Dvora, Lorelie, Anani, Lucky and Apostrophe for making me feel so at home). Thank you Jake Meginsky of Amherst Cinema for insightful and inspiring conversations.

Writing and editing are never a solo undertaking, and this project would be a mess were it not for the following folks who went above and beyond on behalf of this work. I offer the most heartfelt thanks possible to my friend Chris Heller, my dad Jack Butler, gifted colleague and friend Wendy Chen and series editor Shirley Steinberg for reading early, embarrassingly sloppy, drafts. Your individual and collective insight was most helpful; I am properly humbled by your incisive critiques. Thank you, Ivan Forde, for your art–that which graces the cover of this book as well the art that is you. For this, my sophomore effort, Peter Lang's staff, including Bernadette Shade, Phyllis Korper and Chris Myers, proved once again incredibly helpful and responsive. Much respect to the readers and copyeditors who fixed my copious errors. Special thanks to Chris Myers who pays such close attention to me and makes himself available beyond the scope of this project. Any leftover errors are 100% my shortcomings.

Dear friends supported me through this process, without whom I would be lost. Jake, for good and for ill, is always there. Brian showed up just when he was needed, as always. Robert (and Dave and JJ) are thought of and missed daily. Erica Scharrer has been a beacon on this whole journey and her strength, intellect and warmth are inspiring. I'm honored to continue to cross paths in this area of study with Emilie Zaslow–gifted scholar, former classmate and constant friend.

Moments of professional and personal transition often reveal the concept of family on multiple levels, and I'm blessed with a vast extended and chosen family. I thank Joy and Frank, Clark and Carole, sweet Steve, Jon, Hailey (H[1]), Hannah (H[2]) and my amazing and open-hearted outlaw, Angell: A genius, a goddess and the definition of awesome. Aunt Margaret keeps me grounded and entertained with fantastic stories. Kevin read early drafts and engaged in helpful (and sometimes wonderfully inappropriate) conversations. Much love to my new Massachusetts family, the Hanleys, including Janice, Tom, Rachael and the amazing Julia. This crew showed me around, made me feel welcome, literally cared for me when I was sick and invited me into their adventures, of which I love every minute. I feel continuously blessed by Alysia, Aviva, Zale and Ted. Chris, Sherry, Lisa, Celena and Aviva: My girls, though we are far apart, you remain my sisters and my heart-family; the miles have made me love you even more.

I must thank my family of origin, without whom I would not be able to recognize the gift of extended family. My siblings and in-laws Stephanie, Andrew, Jennifer & Jim, Christopher & Jennifer are a formidable support. Special thanks to Team Andrew & Jasmin who help make Massachusetts a phenomenal place to live. Jacob, Eva, Sarah, Jasmin, Charlotte and Annabelle remind me regularly that there is beauty in the world. My dad is my toughest critic, blissfully balanced by my mom, my biggest supporter; I am thankful every day for both of you. Last, but certainly not least, I thank my two most special guys: Sancho and Andy. Sancho, your willingness to stay by my side through all our adventures is all I need in the world. That being said, thanks for allowing Andy to be a part of our family. Andy, thank you for everything (especially always making the time for me to read); you are my true love.

Finding Youth,
Framing Their Reflections

In August 2011, about to enter his senior year at a public university in upstate
New York, Popcorn,[1] a young African American man from Harlem, muses on
his transition to adulthood as we chat on Facebook:

> At this stage in my life where I'm growing into manhood, of course I'm gonna
> question my masculinity, just look at it and really critique it and what I'm do-
> ing, what I'm supposed to do and question that. What is a man supposed to do,
> you know what I mean? And why? And where is that all coming from? It's just a
> massive critique on masculinity, my childhood growing up and doing mad boy
> things. And then seeing and looking at the things I do now. Because I don't re-
> ally look at sports all the time and I'm mostly reading. And I'm like wait, is that
> a masculine thing? Like, how am I supposed to feel about that? How are other
> people supposed to feel about that? It's weird because I don't really participate in
> typical masculine activities. You know what I mean? In my literature classes it's
> mostly girls, in my classes I'm usually one of two or three dudes.

As Popcorn starts to see himself as an adult, admittedly an adult sheltered by the
comforts of full-time college enrollment, he draws on the years we have known
each other as he articulates his development and growth. When I first interviewed
Popcorn, in 2007, he discussed his boyhood and experience with masculinity:

> A boy is still learning. You're not fully experienced. I mean, you're still learning
> when you're a man, but as you move onto manhood, when you reach manhood,

that's like the ultimate level that you can reach, okay, then you just learn from there on.

In the intervening years between the first interview, when Popcorn was a senior in high school, and the most recent as he is about to enter his senior year in college, Popcorn's articulation and ability to express himself and his concerns–his critiques, as he phrases them–have grown profoundly. How? What happened in those intervening years that influenced Popcorn's growth as a human being, as a man, as a scholar?

What happened was that Popcorn graduated from high school, started college, spent a semester studying in Paris, watched his two very best friends sever their friendship, experienced a couple of serious relationships with young women, experimented with drugs, discovered Dostoyevsky, honed his photography, videography and drawing skills and spent much time in the university library on Friday nights. In the grand scheme of things, Popcorn's experience is ordinary; however, when looked at closely, it is an extraordinary life filled with remarkable moments. When carefully analyzed, Popcorn's experiences are deeply political, representing his shift from adolescence to adulthood in an increasingly tumultuous global culture. One of the things that makes his story extraordinary—and the stories of the 19 other young people who are the focal point of this text–is that they all grow up, graduate high school and move into college or work environments accompanied by the digital companion Facebook, which, if nothing else, shifts our method of communication with each other.

In a time of intersecting systems of education, the media and the orthodoxies of neoliberalism, we need to be aware of where young people are in order to explore how individuals maneuvering within these intersections live and grow. What role do young people, perched at the moment of transition from high school to college/work, play in this complex and complicated environment? How do young people reflect and make meaning from the past while living in the present and working towards a productive, fulfilling future? A better understanding of young people and their stake as developing citizens is needed and can be achieved by exploring them over time and through their everyday environments. Young people develop themselves and, in turn, express that development as they grow into adults. This development deserves further exploration.

The seminal research of critical cultural studies focused on youth cultures and explored where young people were in space and time. The research of Stuart Hall and Tony Jefferson, Dick Hebdige, Angela McRobbie and Paul Willis provided the foundation for understanding young people as political bodies that move through and actively influence their surroundings, rather than solely being acted upon.[2] Their work uncovered the extraordinary qualities of ordinary life and emphasized the political importance of personal choices. In this postmillennial time and space, scholars of youth must recommit to finding young people where they are in order to best understand and make meaning of their unique concerns and changes. At this time, young people are found in the digital realm, socializing and connecting through Facebook. They use the digital partly to extrapolate on their experiences in the physical world. As the young people in this text show, their use of Facebook is perceived and discussed as a regular part of their daily lives, a normal, taken-for-granted method of communication. Scholars of youth must find their way to the digital realm in order to make sense of young people's experiences with multiple physical realms.

This text begins by locating multiple crossroads in order to make the case for what is interesting and worth exploring about young people's development through high school and into college and work. The text situates itself in the important, challenging and rich moments of transition between adolescence and adulthood. In present-day America, there is a seemingly unavoidable meeting of systems of schooling and neoliberalism that serve to subjugate young people who do not possess the social capital or invisible privilege to carry them through difficult times. In this text, this impasse is overlaid onto the crossroads of feminist qualitative data gathering and the increasing popularity of social networking sites as an underexplored method of data gathering. Facebook is a firmly grounded part of the digital media environment that is, at the present moment, a vital and accessible way to reach young people in the place where they are most frequently found. The primary data here are the stories of young people gathered over the course of four years through both in-person and electronic interviews. This text is not *about* Facebook, nor is its goal an exploration of how young people *make use* of Facebook. Rather, I use Facebook as a data-gathering site. Though I do share how young people make sense of Facebook and what they do with it, my primary use of Facebook is as for observation and data gathering.

Majoring in Change focuses on how young people reflect on their urban education experiences and make sense of life at pivotal moments of change, using data gathered through in-person interviews and mobile, digital media, especially Facebook. The work follows 20 young people from New York City as they graduate from high school and make the transition to college or work.[3] It focuses on their formal education in high school and college classrooms as well as their informal education expressed through Facebook, where young people digitally congregate and share their experiences daily. Despite concerns about young people interacting with strangers online, research has shown that young people mostly "friend" people they already know in their social world.[4] Facebook provides a digital space to build identity, to comment on the structures of society and to be vulnerable with a trusted population of "friends" who, because of life changes, may no longer be geographically available. Furthermore, friends from a more secure/less transitional time may be called upon in challenging times regardless of geographic location and with little to no perceived cost. Joining Facebook is free (provided one has a high-speed Internet connection or a smartphone with a generous data plan); it uses no cellphone minutes nor does it incur any long-distance charges. Connecting with friends via Facebook has no travel costs or restrictions. Friendships can be formed globally, irrespective of education, work or geography. Facebook connections *feel* infinite in a time when many traditional connections feel fraught. Facebook invites users to explore the world from the safety of their personal communication devices. One important difference between my first interview with Popcorn in which he predicted what adult male life would be like and the second, in which he describes how he sees masculinity now, is the first interview was conducted in person and the second on Facebook. In the years between 2007 and 2011, Popcorn and the other participants have engaged with me in in-person private and small group interviews, telephone interviews and, most recently, interviews conducted via the message and chat functions on Facebook.

The participants' stories are the foundation for what they learned and, in turn, took away from their secondary education as they struggled to make meaning and sense of their new environments and new responsibilities. Some of the participants moved out of New York City while others remained, believing that the familiarity of the city provides them the support they need to succeed in unfamiliar environments. Although the majority of participants claim they do not pay attention to politics, their position as bodies within a time of global economic and social changes reveals they are nevertheless impacted by systemic political maneuverings, specifically changes in education, the economy and technology.

Constructions and Changes in Education, Young People and Facebook

Much literature on young people and urban education uses the walls of the classroom or school building as boundaries; this text situates the actual school and the system of school within a broader environment to illustrate how the concept of school operates as a political tool. Peter McLaren (1999) discusses his work within the classroom and his discovery of the "relatively unexpected ramifications of what it means to acquire an education" (p. 2). "School" has never been just about the walls of the classroom; my exploration of the literature and participants' experiences with education aims to reveal the larger ramifications of acquiring an education from the system of schooling. Schools are at a crossroads on a political battlefield: The current pedagogical conversation revolves around the development of charter schools as part of President Obama's Race to the Top educational reform initiative, and the struggles of the higher education system in the face of long-term economic challenges. This book draws on McLaren's and Paulo Freire's (1970/2000) analyses of the willful oppression of subjugated young people by the larger educational system, mapping it against critiques of neoliberalism and its intentional destruction of public education.[5]

Neoliberalism is an economic philosophy enacted in global policy shifts that favor and reward capitalist enterprise,[6] and it is intimately connected to the global market crash of 2008.[7] Neoliberalism serves to deregulate markets by privatizing public goods and services, and it reaches far into socioeconomically struggling communities in desperate need of social services. Increased privatization, charter schools and for-profit enterprise are fertile ground for "venture philanthropists"– individuals who leverage private money to influence public schools, to develop the metaphor of the student and family consumer.[8]

The participants in this study were caught in the crossfire of No Child Left Behind, Race to the Top and the major global economic breakdown that undoubtedly impacted their experience with both education and work. Neoliberalism negatively impacts the public school system and, in turn, puts the university system in a precarious position. The period of transition from high school to college is an underexplored area of study (Arnett 2004; Bloom 2005), particularly for low-income urban students with little to no familial experience with university learning; in this text it is explored in detail. During the time the participants made their transitions, mobile, digital media grew rapidly and gave young people a site for self-expression and (digital) socializing.

This text shares the stories of participants as they make a vital transition in their lives: Out of high school and into college and/or work. Participants' stories are positioned against the language and popular discussion of education in order to illustrate their resilience and growth within a neoliberal environment. The participants in this study who currently attend college believe they were poorly prepared for university learning and their memories of strong interpersonal and family-like connections made in high school reveal a conspicuous absence of the intellectual, social and systemic preparation needed for university learning. Participants who chose not to attend college determined themselves that they were not "college material" and that continued schooling was not worth the financial risk. A deficient high school education has left these young people largely unaware of the political forces that set them up for failure and self-doubt, which, in turn, ready them to be members of a docile workforce. Participants spend a great deal of time on Facebook in large part because it is the place where they can connect most frequently with their peers and family and where they can share their constructions of self. Regular participation on Facebook also invites an escape from the very real pressures of the physical world, including expectations from school, work and family. While Facebook presents itself as a democratic space, it must be more carefully examined to explore what "labor" young people do (for free) within the larger digital media environment. Facebook's founder Mark Zuckerberg's insistence on a vision where all our intersecting interests are shared digitally not-so-subtly masks the work members do on the site to continuously archive data.[9] This book neither celebrates nor castigates Facebook; instead, it recognizes that Facebook is an important part of young people's identity development and deserves close, critical examination.

This text examines young people from a position as close as possible to their natural environment. Because the world of social networking is where many young people spend much of their time, data are gathered from the place where young people are most consistently available. From 2006 to 2008 I worked in curriculum development at Lincoln Square High School[10] (LSHS), a New York City public school whose mission was to apply the study of media to social change. I engaged in quasi-ethnographic participant-observation research and conducted interviews with 21 young people about their understandings of the media, media education and urban education (Butler 2010). Through Facebook, I am still in touch with many of the students I worked with, including several of the initial research participants.

Since 2008, I have conducted electronic and in-person interviews with seven of the original participants and 13 new participants. I chose to conduct Facebook interviews because that is where the young people are found regularly; through private messaging, they can take the time to answer questions, and we develop a long-term dialogue about their progression and changes. Facebook is as yet an unknown entity in terms of validity of data gathering. Facebook invites us to create "fictional personas" that are not lies per se but rather constructions of who we want to be (Roiphe 2010; Turkle 2011). When dealing with young people specifically, particularly those who are involved in a pivotal shift in their personal identity project as they transition out of the relatively protective confines of high school and into the world as independent, self-managing adults, Facebook invites the "fictional, practice self" to develop. There is a marked difference between the thoughtful, critical responses to private interview questions and the near-constant status updates. I do not believe the participants lie to me; rather, they practice the work of developing their multiple selves. Therefore, this text documents in detail the methodological progression, which draws directly from their words and stories mapped against the critical perspectives from research on social networking, digital democracy and identity development.[11]

What's Happening in Education?

In 2009 the writings of several education scholars, intellectuals and students were gathered together in the *Harvard Educational Review*'s issue on Barack Obama and his potential plans for the nation's primary and secondary schools. Most scholars and intellectuals on the Left were in agreement that No Child Left Behind was an outright failure, but what, exactly, Obama would do was still unclear.

Amidst discussions on health-care reform, global war on multiple fronts and continued concern over the state of the economy, Obama spoke about his plans to fix the nation's public schools. What was clear almost immediately was that "fixing" the nation's public schools involved altering the concept of public schooling through the development of a robust charter school system, a plan for mapping test scores against teacher accountability, increased competition among schools, students and staffs, and the increased presence of testing. In Obama's plan, public schools in impoverished urban areas are taken over by private industries and teachers are promoted as the public face of reform as they become employees of private industry. In his effort to make things better, fast, President Obama's Race to the Top initiative will effectively end the public school system as it is currently conceptualized.

In April 2010 the first of the $4.5 billion Race to the Top allotments were distributed to a variety of the nation's public school districts. What this money will actually *do* has yet to be determined, and in the intervening months, education conversations take place in a crowded news environment as increased global turmoil occupies the headlines on the front pages and 24–hour cable news networks. The nation's complex, complicated and extraordinarily messy public schools are making dramatic changes with no guarantee of receiving money and no clear plans for how to effectively spend any received money. More importantly, there is no evidence that the changes they make will have any positive, long-term pedagogical value.

Because the participants are in the midst of moving from high school to college, the Race to the Top changes do not affect them specifically. But this shifting education system that includes the remnants of No Child Left Behind, the proposed changes for Race to the Top and the global economic meltdown, makes it increasingly difficult for all but the wealthiest youth to attend college without incurring crippling debt. The broader narrative impacts the culture as a whole and informs how people think about education. I pay attention to the popular press coverage of education reformers and reform movements, showing how the language used galvanizes aggressive neoliberal action. With Race to the Top and its emphasis on charter school development, increased standardized testing and financial rewards for "great" teachers, the new model of schooling against which the public system will be measured is the charter school. A possible result will be that the nation's public schools will fall into greater disrepair than they already are and students already disadvantaged socially and economically will experience more disadvantages as the charter school model gains popularity. Through the lens of neoliberalism, those young people who do not choose (or are not chosen) to attend charter schools are responsible for their continued struggle. Two things must be made clear: First, there is no "charter school model," despite the language used by politicians and in the popular press; charter schools do not operate with a guiding pedagogy and in decades of development, the only certain thing that can be said about charter schools is that nothing certain is known. Second, there is no clear theory or method of reform grounded by charter schools, thereby making the act of reform little more than political rhetoric.

Overall, President Obama's Race to the Top marks the triumph of free-market ideology that encourages a competition not aligned with the traditional model of public schooling. Education within the free-market paradigm, including increased privatization and corporatization of public schooling, encourages a staggeringly uneven playing field where competition is played out between those prepared for the experience and those ill-prepared for competition. Though it is a relatively recent phenomenon, this style of reform is characterized by remarkably quick growth (Saltman 2005). A neoliberal approach to education was first envisioned by University of Chicago economist Milton Friedman (1955), and leapt in popularity during the Nixon and Reagan administrations.[12] According to Kenneth Saltman (2005), neoliberal education is marked by three intertwined phenomena: the privatization of public schools through funding schemes, the promotion of the voucher system and the development of charter schools; the framing of education debates in economic, rather than public or social, terms; and the reframing of school via a corporate model. Neoliberalism demands that the public have faith in the free market to solve all problems while it scrubs away any ethical difficulties for this belief (Giroux 2010a).

What makes the efforts of neoliberalism successful today is private industry's attraction to disaster. As Saltman (2007b) argues, "around the world, disaster is providing the means for business to accumulate profit" (p. 2). He offers in evidence the Asian tsunami of 2005, the no-bid reconstruction contracts in Iraq and Afghanistan, and the wholesale privatization of New Orleans' public schools after Hurricane Katrina. This predatory form of educational privatization appears, on the surface, altruistic (schools are built quickly), yet there are nefarious goals: Specifically, the privatization of schools for corporate interests, which, in turn, transforms the citizen into a consumer and reimagines the public sphere as the free market. While it might at first appear philanthropic that large corporations with expendable capital rebuild areas struck by disaster, Pepi Leistyna (2007) warns this predatory behavior needs closer examination. Most disasters are largely "products of human negligence, indifference, greed and structural suffering" and neoliberalism drops in as a way to further dissolve governments' role in social services (p. 141).

The immersion of private industry into education is found in the language applied to pedagogical training and school reform. Saltman (2007b) observes that terms such as "achievement, excellence, and best practices" are borrowed from the business world without clarification of their intent or definition when translated into the language of pedagogy (p. 13). For example, Michael Klonsky (Ayers &

Klonsky 2007) points out how the word "autonomy," long used to mean "teachers having more control over their teaching, over the teaching and learning environment," has been manipulated to now "give freedom to private management companies to run schools in ways that fail to serve all kids" (p. 181). This language is borrowed, in part, because these are largely unemotional terms that can be applied to highly emotional issues. The unemotional terms also serve to mask the work that happens behind the scenes as private industry reorganizes public institutions in the face of disaster. In conversation with each other, William Ayers and Klonsky (2007) discuss the role of disaster in promoting private industry. Klonsky observes that the "politics of disaster" have been used to erode public space and public ownership "in order to justify closing public schools, turning them over to private management companies" in the belief that public schools (indeed, all public institutions) work poorly *because* they are public; the only solution (provided and publicized) is private industry (p. 177).

President Obama's language reveals his belief in the efficacy of private industry. In July 2009 he linked the need to heal education with the economic stimulus package. Obama spoke then, as he does today, about creating jobs, opening credit markets and extending social service benefits. One important way to make space for these things to blossom and flourish is to make schools better. He constructed knowledge as a material good to be traded, calling it "the most valuable commodity a person and a country have to offer" and declaring that the future "belongs to the nation that best educates its people" (Obama 2009).

Why Facebook?

The 2010 film *The Social Network* (Fincher), based on the book *The Accidental Billionaires* (Mezrich 2009) about the development of Facebook and the interpersonal, social and pecuniary turmoil connected with the site's rise, focuses on the ultimate social value: Being important. Facebook creator Zuckerberg is portrayed as an unlikable computer geek who is able to hack Harvard's network in one night in order to enact revenge on a girl who broke up with him earlier that evening. While both the film and the book on which it was based take romantic liberties, an important truth is revealed and documented: In order to feel important (or, at least, feel less unimportant), people must live their lives in public. To make one's life public, absent celebrity, one must have a digital presence.

One vital theme throughout the film is the perpetual adolescence enabled by Facebook. Although it seems at first that with a digital presence all facets of one's life are on display, in actuality, secrets and fears can be hidden in plain sight. The implication of the final scene of the film, where Zuckerberg impatiently waits for the young woman scorned to "friend" him, is that his whole business venture was concocted as an attempt to win back this one woman. Facebook now famously enables users to construct a persona of who they want to be without technically lying, which is not so dissimilar from adolescents "trying on" various identities. The popular press regularly laments the dangers to young people (and threats made *by* young people) that the digital environment enables (McCabe 2010; Richtel 2010). These are exotic, rare acts that are more titillating than the banal activities of the average daily user checking in and being checked on by peers and family members. Digital, mobile media and social networking are now firmly entrenched in the larger mainstream media landscape; Facebook clearly illustrates this arc, having surrendered the exclusivity of being accessible only to those with an @harvard.edu email address and now reaching more than 750 million people across the globe (Facebook.com 2011, *Statistics*). If using Facebook is akin to prolonging adolescence, Facebook itself is now the most popular kid in class, working diligently to maintain its status.

What follows, then, is that it is necessary to continue to build critical scholarship on what Facebook is and how it is situated in the larger cultural landscape. A continued debate within studies of youth and media is what the media *do to* young people and what, in turn, young people *do with* the media (Buckingham 2000; Butler 2011). At the center of this debate is the trace fear of the unknown, especially the digital unknown. To study Facebook is to adopt an anthropological perspective (Geertz 1983) where the digital is explored as a site of cultural relevance that must be observed and interrogated; the challenge is how to critique the environment from a distance while simultaneously being a part of that environment. This book uses Facebook as a data-gathering site and critiques the larger media environment that includes Facebook to tease out some of the ways in which its most frequent users use the site as they make a particularly important transition in their lives. My hope is that, through the participants' stories, a better understanding of the current state of affairs may be achieved.

Meeting the Participants

Aged 18 to 21, the participants are at the first official point of change as adults. Though many of them have experienced significant hardships and have undoubtedly worked through many "adult" experiences, within the boundaries of mainstream society, they are only now "officially" adults. Therefore, I begin by examining the tangible structures where young people are found as they progress from adolescence to adulthood: High school, college and work.

This text opens with a discussion of the literature on the current shifts in public education, particularly Race to the Top, charter schools and increased pressures in the university and labor market. With reference to McLaren's (1999) and Freire's (1970/2000) arguments that "education" and "schooling" are bigger and more complex than the classrooms in which they unfold, I explore the literature critical of neoliberalism and its pervasive influence on public schooling.[13] The participants attended a start-up high school whose rhetoric promised a unique, rigorous education but actually left the majority of them largely unprepared for life after high school. While personal responsibility absolutely must be accounted for, so must the school take responsibility for lulling students into the belief they were ready for the challenges faced after graduation.

This pivotal shift from high school to college/work means little without young people's stories on the process. Chapter Two explores the methodology of this research, introducing the participants and how their stories about their transitions were collected. For several years now, Facebook has been an extraordinarily popular social networking site, especially with young people. Social networking shifts social and interpersonal interactions and yet remains an understudied part of both the mass media and its role in qualitative data gathering. Young people spend a great deal of time on Facebook, posting frequent newsfeed updates and creating a platform to introduce their presence on Twitter, Tumblr, YouTube, Formspring and other social media sites. They do not do this only from home computers or even the more mobile laptops. Smartphones and video game consoles enable the near-constant updates from any geographic location. For all its freedom, however, Facebook is not an unblemished haven for digital democracy. Social networking fosters an illusory digital democracy that presents itself as a site to cultivate individual power and self-control for young people, but in fact it subsumes them further into the corporate media conglomerate.

Despite this, scholars who engage in qualitative research have not tackled Facebook as a data environment. The primary data for *Majoring in Change* are drawn from the stories of 20 young men and women who have graduated from high school and now attend college or strive to find full-time work. The data were gathered over the span of four years via in-person and electronic interviews. One of the founding tenets of feminist qualitative data gathering (McRobbie 1982/1991), particularly with in-depth interviews, is to reach out to participants in their natural environments to create an accurate and complex picture of their lives. If we want to better understand and make thorough sense of young people from within their environments, we must reach out to Facebook as a research tool.

Participants reflect on high school and its purpose, discuss their transition to college and work and prepare for their futures. The primary data draw from the perspectives gained over time and through multiple experiences to show how young people articulate their experiences and the lessons they have learned along the way. Chapter Three invites participants to reflect on what they remember from high school and whether they felt prepared for life after high school. Chapter Four focuses on what young people believe is the purpose of high school, especially as they progress beyond it and use their knowledge as the foundation of their new experiences. Chapter Five explores how young people make meaning of the points of transition in their lives. Chapter Six attends to the stories of Genevieve and Popcorn, two students who chose to attend college immediately after high school and had vastly different experiences in their respective transitions. Genevieve and Popcorn tell very different stories, but in their years out of high school and into college they carved their own paths, acknowledged their struggles and worked to create spaces in which they feel successful.

A Call for Media Literacy

As we move into the second decade of the 21st century, it seems that less, not more, is known about young people, advancements in the media and developments in education. I will argue that a critical media literacy intervention is needed: Young people, their teachers and scholars of youth deserve focused critical attention to the sweeping changes in education and technologies that impact their lives. The critical cultural studies literature that taught where young people were, what mattered to them, and how they could be understood as political bodies grows increasingly pertinent again. We live in uncertain times that demand complex solutions with careful thought and application. What on the surface appears easy and free–social networking as enabled by digital, mobile media–is a major agent of change that has been explored only superficially.

Critical media literacy draws on young people who are deeply and regularly engaged with the media. The media, especially the popular press, deliver contradictory messages about who young people are, what their schools look like and how their futures can be imagined. In the mainstream media there are few opportunities for young people to speak on their own behalf and be heard by policy makers. Advances in mobile, digital media may provide a space for young people to express themselves, but if they are not taught the skills of critical inquiry, if they are not shown how they matter and how their individual actions and choices are a part of the larger civic society, they may not see the purpose of contributing their views. As this research will show, most participants do not pay much attention to broad civic issues in part because they see no connection to themselves, and they believe that the people in charge are committed to lies rather than the truth. The participants are so weary of decisions being made without their input that they are no longer interested in investing the energy needed to make critical sense of the world they face. Instead of seeing politics and choices made in the name of political growth as remote or unimportant, students of critical media literacy can use the media to make more informed, analytic contributions while reflecting on their own development and responsibility.

Throughout this text, I will point out specific places where critical inquiry is lacking and where it will be helpful; I conclude with a discussion of why, based on the stories of the participants, critical media literacy should be a valuable part of school reform and how it should be envisioned. In order to better understand young people, the media and education, scholars of youth must recommit to exploring where young people are, what their social and political stakes are in the changing media landscape, and how these changes are felt and contribute to their education. It is a goal of this book to contribute to that necessary dialogue.

ONE

Public Education
and the Private Interest

In his exploration of the class and quality divisions within the institution of the school, Paulo Freire (1970/2000) argued that subjugated bodies, once divided, appear complacent to their divisions. Similarly, Peter McLaren's (1999) exploration of school as ritual works to disrupt and re-mark themes in education through a more thorough understanding of the construct of education and its role in political economy. What happens when those divided are increasingly separated by political upheavals and global tumult?

The eldest of the participants in this study graduated from high school on the cusp of great economic and political unrest, which has grown more chaotic in the intervening years. The graduates of 2008 finished high school just months before the global economic collapse and at the end of President Bush's second term. They began college or looked for jobs in a time of economic struggle and political change, which undoubtedly impacted their experiences. The 2009 and 2010 graduates completed high school amidst this change and entered college or work in even greater uncertainty. Despite the chaos lived within the walls of their high school, the majority of participants were decidedly unprepared for the chaos of the real world beyond those walls. They were unwittingly complacent to the familiarity of chaos and assumed that familiarity would continue.

The participants saw their already difficult lives become increasingly difficult in the face of economic collapse, and many battled with a tenuous grasp on their goals. Some believe there is no point to college because it delays opportunities to make money even as they struggle at part-time jobs with little money, no security and no room for advancement. This chapter discusses the broad changes to the American secondary school and university systems within the frame of the 2008 economic collapse, the changes promised by the Obama administration and the increased adherence to the orthodoxies of neoliberalism that influence education.

There is no singular reason *why* American public secondary schools are as entangled as they are. Journalists, scholars and public intellectuals discuss reasons as varied as how money is spent, what education is for, the job teachers do and what role policy plays. Journalist Amanda Ripley (2008) observes that despite the fact that more money is spent per pupil, American children consistently fall behind their global peers in large part because of "ineffective teaching." Education scholar Linda Darling-Hammond (2010) believes that U.S. schools have lost focus on multiple levels, including lack of attention to teacher training, distracting curriculum wars and concentration on creating schools not designed for 21st century changes. Henry Giroux (2003, 2009b, 2010b) and Kenneth Saltman (2007b, 2010) argue that schools fail students because of oppressive policies that disempower the most vulnerable students and, by default, ensure the security and well-being of those already privileged.

What Darling-Hammond (2010) names our "continuing comfort with profound inequality" (p. 8) marks the current face of school struggle and reform. Despite the glaring problems in schools, overall there is a tacit acceptance of the variables as inevitable. The United States spends a great deal of money on education, but does not make that money work productively for all students within the school system. This is largely because of a continued, though unsubstantiated, faith in free-market principles. Other countries that spend less per student on education see greater advancements, in large part because money allotted to education is spent *on education*. In the United States, money allotted to education is used for a host of social services not generally supported by federal policy, particularly for impoverished youth. Including social services in basic care means schools focus on schooling; in the United States, school is often responsible for the mental, physical, emotional and nutritional health of children. While this is to be lauded, and has undoubtedly worked to the benefit of countless students, it puts a great burden on one single institution to take care of a host of needs. Darling-Hammond (2010) argues this is a result of conservative policy reforms made during Reagan's presidency that "focused on outcome rather than input," when policy makers started looking to high-stakes testing as the measure of success (pp. 20–21). The "outcome rather than input" belief is the crux of neoliberal orthodoxies, which, while often blatantly obvious, are sometimes hidden in plain sight. For example, Harlem Children's Zone, Geoffrey Canada's plan to care for the whole child from birth to college, illustrates how much money is needed to bolster impoverished communities–money not available in the local community.[1]

Canada struggled to open schools in his Harlem community, making promises that remained unfulfilled for several years. What he ultimately chose to do was operate his schools more like businesses, thereby capitulating to free-market desires. Canada received money from private businesses that reframed the community schools in the interest of for-profit industry. In an environment marked by the conspicuous absence of funds, a promise of surplus funds is hard to resist. Canada's experience is an example of the current changes in secondary education. As public schools increasingly are taken over by private interests, the purpose of public education, and whom it serves, must be further explored.

What Is [Public] Education for?

The ideal purpose of school is to prepare the present generation for the future, for active participation and citizenship in a democracy. By the mid-20th century most American children attended school full-time, earning a high school diploma (Ravitch 1983). Formal schooling largely replicated young people's social and cultural capital: Poor children, especially poor children of color, received a mediocre education that prepared them for mediocre jobs, while privileged children received a privileged education. In this way, class divisions were maintained and strengthened (Freire 1970/2000). Post–Civil Rights movement suburban schools developed with a predominantly white and privileged student body. The suburban public school flourished in large part because schools were paid for primarily through property taxes, and wealthier, more privileged communities built well-funded, high-quality schools. Poor, dispossessed communities, in contrast, made do with poorly funded, disintegrating schools. A gulf developed between the quality of these schools, and despite decades of rhetoric promising change, little has demonstrably changed. Rural and urban public school systems faltered for a number of years; most notably struggles in New York City, Chicago and Washington, D.C. were well known.[2] Urban schools worked diligently to match the success of suburban schools, where a variety of emergency reforms were tested, including formation of small schools, decreased student-teacher ratios, increased school hours per day, increased days per year, theme-centered learning, and introduction of uniforms and discipline measures, to name but a smattering.[3] When local community-based public schools seemed beyond repair, vouchers and charters became popular.[4] All these changes occurred while educators admitted that schools served different students differently. For privileged youth in highly functional public secondary schools, education was preparation for college. For underprivileged youth in dysfunctional public secondary schools, education became increasingly a route to the military or menial jobs (Giroux 2009b, 2010b).

At the turn to the 21st century, with a work environment shifting away from industry towards technology-focused digital labor and increased global competition, education as preparation took on a new significance and became increasingly divided between intellectual and job preparation. Many scholars on the Left are opposed to education as "merely" job training and employment preparation.[5] Saltman (2005) defends public schools as the place where students gain knowledge and learn to use tools "to comprehend and criticize social injustices and to develop capacities to imagine and enact a better world together with other citizens," which he contrasts with a corporate vision that "imagines students as developing workers and consumers" (pp. 194–195). Saltman (2005) queries the worth of corporate labor readiness at the expense of an informed, critically engaged citizenry. Whether this was ever the intent of public schools, schooling is definitely at a crossroads of shifting labor readiness, location and expectation. However, Saltman (2007b) continues to caution against the vision of public school as a "tool of a capitalist state and economy" (p. 14). The language of job preparation hides the goal of preparing the most privileged youth for high-skilled careers and continuing to replicate the docile workforce in working-class populations.

Similar concerns play out in higher education. Giroux (2010a) writes that the responsibility of higher education is to "teach students how to be responsive to the conflicts of our times, identify antidemocratic forces in the wider society, and connect knowledge, power, and critical modes of agency to the task of imagining a more just world while demonstrating a willingness to struggle for it." In the face of economic, technological and global change, higher education's priorities have shifted. Higher education, like secondary education, reacts to the pressures on the economy and the technology-focused labor environment, capitulating to a free-market ethos. Yes, education must be flexible enough to change with larger social and cultural shifts, but what remains unknown is what these changes look like, in whose interest they will be made and whose benefit will be of primary concern. Darling-Hammond (2010) writes, "the new mission of schools is to prepare students to work at jobs that do not yet exist, creating ideas and solutions for products and problems that have not yet been identified, using technologies that have not been invented" (p. 2). Not knowing the future means there is great opportunity, which raises the question: Great opportunity for whom and with what vision?

Ethnic minorities, poverty and education

In the history of public schooling in America, poor children of color have long served as a site of conflict between rhetoric and action. Young people in general have unwittingly played the conflicting roles of promise of the future or proof of future demise (Buckingham 2000; Giroux 2003). More contentiously, impoverished youth of color from urban areas have played these roles while facing a litany of struggles and conflicts. Impoverished youth are criticized as "undisciplined, morally and intellectually immature, overly emotional, hypersexual, and lacking in self-control" (Gillen 2009, p. 364). Simultaneously, impoverished youth lack access to the resources that will help them make positive changes (Darling-Hammond 2010; De Leon 2006). Education is believed to be the most successful route to productive change, yet impoverished youth are denied access to exemplary schools. High concentrations of poverty have a negative impact on the well-being of all students, including non-poor students. Inexperienced teachers are hired in high-poverty schools, and schools with predominantly African American and Latino youth are provided weaker curricula, fewer materials and an unhealthy school environment (Darling-Hammond 2010; Giroux 2010b).

Academic achievement–or failure–is cumulative, and lower-class and impoverished youth experience an achievement gap *before* they get to school, which widens when they are in school. In a large-scale study on the achievement gap, Tamara Wilder, Whitney Allgood and Richard Rothstein (2008) argue that reform dollars are wasted because policy makers place "nearly exclusive emphasis on reforming schools," thereby ignoring the breadth of struggle faced by the lower classes beyond the classroom. Because of lack of access to social services that bolster healthy development, poor students miss a great deal of school, setting them further behind from very early on. Wilder, Allgood and Rothstein argue that policy changes thus far have played "catch-up" to pre-existing conditions. In order to make demonstrable change in the lives of poor children, policy makers must shift their starting point. Geoffrey Canada's aim to raise the whole child by making changes to all aspects of the environment clearly works to minimize this conspicuous gap (Tough 2008), yet the reliance on private industry means the community and government abdicate responsibility. When "someone else" solves the problem, that "someone else" cannot be held accountable for how they choose to do so especially when "someone else" is private industry that does not have to make public their activities. Putting reform dollars directly into schools *looks* good but does not necessarily tackle the larger issues, and when schools do not make immediate, positive change, private industry again points out the ineffectiveness of the public sphere.

When more money is put directly into schools, and no corresponding money is given to health, wellness or social services, young people continue to run the risk of missing school, possibly setting them even further behind. Currently, non-profit–and increasingly, for-profit–private enterprises are interested in reforming public schools. Individuals with strong private business backgrounds but little to no experience in classrooms believe there is a better way to teach poor children. Knowledge Universe, Teach for America, Harlem Children's Zone, the Edison Schools and the Knowledge Is Power Program (KIPP) are some of the better-known educational enterprises. As Saltman (2002) observes, these "lifelong learning" companies "seek to reinvent the school on the model of the corporation" (p. 238). Many of these companies were started by individuals with little to no understanding of pedagogy or by enthusiastic but inexperienced teachers who wanted to create radical change right away. Former Washington, D.C. schools chancellor Michelle Rhee worked for Teach for America before she determined she could do more good outside the classroom (Brown 2008). After her three years as schools chancellor, she runs her own educational consulting firm focused on how to improve schools (Banchero 2011). Two young teachers with big ideas started the KIPP schools in the belief that the school day should be longer and discipline (in the form of being nice and polite to each other) should be the classroom emphasis (Mathews 2009). In Harlem, Geoffrey Canada began Harlem Children's Zone with a vision to change the community in its entirety. He believed the gaps between school and family, health, learning and labor to be too vast (Tough 2008). The holistic approach taken by Canada relies on the business model of privatizing public education. The schools within Harlem Children's Zone are charter schools and Canada's primary funders are business associates. Indeed, Canada himself believes "a business model was the exact right approach for Promise Academy, and for his entire organization" (Tough, p. 135).

Simultaneously, college grows more expensive, often beyond reach for middle- and working-class families and impossible for impoverished families. It is not unheard of for tuition to be "three times [a] family's income" (Bloom 2005, p. 68). Poor and working-class children who attended secondary schools with inadequate college preparation have less access to college, and when they are able to attend college, must balance work and family responsibilities that make focusing primarily on classwork impossible. Within the continued economic struggle, Giroux (2009b) observes that poor and working-class youth restricted from college are solidified as "redundant and expendable" (p. 110). As young people struggle to attend college, *what* college they attend perpetuates class divisions. Giroux (2009b) notes American higher education is increasingly "divided into those institutions that educate the elite to rule the world in the twenty-first century and the second- and third-tier institutions that largely train students for low-paid positions in the capitalist world economy" (p. 116). The practice of education, irrespective of rhetoric, perpetuates class divisions, further strengthening those already primed for success and leaving the rest to become part of the machine.

Ideally, school should develop the citizens of a nation and enable growth in both intellectual and labor abilities. In their scathing critiques of the current face of education reform, Kenneth Saltman, Henry Giroux and William Ayers lament the annihilation of an informed, active citizenry, replaced by a docile workforce. Ayers (2009) writes, "the promise of education is always tied up with the radical proposition that we can change our lives right now, today" (p. 389). This promise, he argues, is a particularly urgent one in a democratic society because democracy is dynamic. Public school is the place to foster public debate in a noncommercial environment, and when it is privatized by for-profit enterprise, critical thinking is inherently limited by the strictures of private industry.[6] When public education is built on the model of private industry, students have two possible roles: Buyer or seller (Giroux 2009a). Impoverished youth of color are limited to the position of buyer, but given the current state of the economy, they are further relegated to the sidelines because of their inability to purchase.

College education: Social, financial and political struggle

A college education was once a rare choice for young people to pursue. Over the years, especially as the United States has shifted from an industry-based society to a knowledge- and, increasingly, technology-based society, college has become a necessity for most American youth (Arnett 2004). Louis Menard (2011) writes about two theories on the purpose of a college education. The first theory sees college as a sorting mechanism for the nation's brightest youth; the second sees college as a place where young people are exposed to information beyond their comfort zones. The accessibility of a college education has varied considerably over time. Menard points out that Harvard University, arguably the nation's most elite, competitive university, had an 85% acceptance rate in 1940; by 2010, the acceptance rate was 6%. In 1950, about 1.4 million people attended public universities whereas today, about 15 million do. In the United States, about 68% of high school graduates attend college, up from about 49% in 1980. The United States has an extensive higher education system with more than 4,000 colleges, universities and community colleges, which Jeffrey Arnett (2004) argues offers young people "abundant opportunities to obtain higher educations that will allow them to explore a wide range of possible occupational futures" (p. 120). U.S. labor and industry value a college education; a college degree is a requirement for entry-level professional jobs, and it is a goal of all secondary schools to have students adequately prepared for college upon high school graduation (though, as will be discussed, it remains unclear what, precisely, "prepared" means).

For students, college matriculation is a pivotal moment of transition marked by increased personal freedoms (and corresponding responsibilities). For families, college is about increased expenses not matched simultaneously by increased income. The transition to college can be exciting, while also fraught with increased personal responsibility. For young people who leave home for college, the absence of a parent/guardian monitoring their daily activities means there are greater opportunities for risk-associated behaviors. Kim Fromme, William Corbin and Marc Kruse (2008) explored risk-taking behaviors, including underage drinking, illegal drug use and promiscuous sexual behavior in more than 2,000 students and found the high school to college transition a particularly evocative time. They posit that a majority of college students move away from home to live on or near campus, which means young people find themselves "in an environment where direct supervision of their behaviors is typically limited and opportunities to engage in a variety of behavioral risks (e.g., heavy alcohol use, casual sex) are often abundant" (p. 1497). Overall, they found few significant differences in gender or socioeconomic status, but white students "reported greater involvement in all behavioral risks except having multiple sexual partners" (p. 1501). The authors believe that "decreased adult supervision, overall greater personal freedom, and increased availability and opportunity are likely contributors to the increases observed for drinking, marijuana use, and sexual behavior" (p. 1501). The balance of freedom versus responsibility may be too much for some young people to handle, and learning self-control and self-discipline can be overwhelming, leading to increased risk-associated behaviors (Arnett 2004).

A college degree remains a necessary requirement for most entry-level professional jobs despite disheartening rates of college attendance, graduation and employment.[7] Only half the students who begin college receive a four-year degree in large part because of rising costs and less money available for aid (Taylor 2010), and one-quarter drop out during their first year (Arnett 2004). African American and Latino students drop out of college at a higher rate than white students, possibly because more African Americans and Latinos grow up in impoverished communities, attend poor schools, and have greater financial burdens than the majority of white students (Arnett). Young people interested in college may have to choose between less expensive public colleges or no college at all. Decreased enrollments means schools that rely on tuition dollars are in a more precarious position, forced to raise tuitions that their students already cannot afford—a vicious and seemingly unsolvable cycle. Private tuition can easily be $20,000 to $40,000 a year, a prohibitive cost for many families,[8] and elite universities can be as much as $200,000 for four years (Taylor).[9] With only 19% of the class of 2009 graduating with jobs (Taylor) and 35.3% of 2008 graduates underemployed (Matgouranis & Robe 2010), it is easy to understand how a four-year degree can feel fruitless, especially for families struggling financially. In a letter to college students, Barbara Ehrenreich (2007) questions whether college is worth it for any but the most financially stable students. She writes:

> On average, you will graduate with a respectable-sized debt of $20,000, which will enable you to establish your all-important 'credit history.' If we have succeeded in our educational mission, you will be a first-rate debtor, capable of making minimum monthly payments much of the time. As fresh offers of credit cards and home equity loans pour in, you will beam with pride at your achievement.

All that money may once have been justified by the value of a college education, but that, too, has suffered. Those who study college pedagogy cannot articulate precisely *what* students are learning or when, in their four years, they will learn it.[10] Furthermore, increasing numbers of students are graduating from high school unprepared for college-level study. Data from New York State revealed that less than half of students in the state were prepared for college (Otterman 2011b). The combination of poor intellectual preparation coupled with increased stress from the recession may be the reasons why the health of college freshmen is the poorest it has been in the 25 years since measurement began (Lewin 2011).

Education and the Obama Administration

The 2008 election of Barack Obama came with the promise of hope and commitment to change. Scholars on the Left greeted Obama's election with cautious optimism,[11] and while there was no evidence that he would make progressive changes in education, there was certainly an abiding hope. Darling-Hammond (2009), who worked closely with Obama during the campaign to craft his educational platform, writes that Obama sought much advice regarding "the development of a strong teaching profession, math and science education, citizenship and encouragement of a service ethic, access to college and support for at-risk students to prevent dropping out and to get kids back in school" (p. 211). While Giroux (2009a) gave credit to Obama for his desire to undo many of the injustices of the previous administration, he cautioned that the administration would "fail badly if it does not connect the current financial and credit meltdown to the inherited crisis of democracy and education—both of which have been undermined by market ideologies for decades" (p. 251). Obama did connect education to the financial collapse, though not in the way progressive scholars had hoped. Given his ties with centrist business organizations, it was unsurprising when Obama's educational plans turned out to be in line with private industry. Obama's plan for reform strengthens neoliberalism's hold on education.

Neoliberalism and the corporatization of public education

While the Obama administration makes promises to change the face of public schooling, it has departed from the progressive agenda that marked his campaign. Giroux (2009a) points out the contradictions inherent in Obama's emphasizing austerity measures in business while expanding market-driven protocols in education. Obama's educational advisors have business backgrounds, and they point him in the direction of the free market and private enterprise. The most broad and far-reaching change to the public school system is its increased corporatization and privatization. Free-market reformers make changes in favor of public industry while working to dismantle teacher professionalism and protection. Competition, choice and incentives are introduced in the interest of increased privatization.

The corporatization of public schooling is captained by educational management organizations (EMOs). EMOs run public schools for profit by drawing from tax money and private funding to start and maintain schools in the private interest. Corporations have become increasingly interested in education because there is rich opportunity for profit and, more insidiously, an opportunity to craft a disciplined workforce "willing to submit to wage labor and the organization of time and work by others in positions of authority" (Saltman 2005, p. 4). Ideological arguments claim that the private sector can better handle the struggles faced in schools. EMOs counter the mission of the democratized public school with an increased emphasis on testing, scripted lessons and prefabricated curricula that can be purchased ready-made. Teachers become data-pushers rather than facilitators of learning and critical inquiry. This decreases opportunities for students "to learn to ask critical questions, raise public concerns, engage in democracy and how it relates to life in a democratic society" (Saltman 2005, p. 11). As private industries, EMOs need not follow standard public school models. Corporations spin this as innovativeness, but, in reality, there is no transparency in curriculum development and no public information on the school-corporation relationship (Bulkley 2004). The absence of transparency means young people and their families are less involved in the process of schooling. Private industry defends itself as working in the best interest of the students and as being more streamlined than public education bureaucracies.

While private corporations may indeed be more streamlined than the bureaucracy that marks many public school systems across the nation, schools are not businesses; when they are treated as such, critical thinking is manipulated and the public nature of public schools is diluted. Schools run by private industry are not open to public scrutiny (Bracey 2002), and communities grow increasingly less informed. When neoliberalism operates as a predator, the community becomes prey.

Despite the promises of the market, neoliberalism has done little to improve education for the nation's most struggling youth. The economic logic of the free market does not translate to the real work needed in classrooms (Buckley & Schneider 2007; Butler 2010). Ultimately, neoliberalism works to systematically undo democracy and the democratic classroom. Its role in educational reform has, Saltman (2010) argues, "deeply authoritarian tendencies that are incompatible with democracy" (p. 25). One of the most conspicuous and far-reaching results of neoliberalism is the increased attention to and development of charter schools.

Charter schools

One prominent result of the corporatization of schooling is the increased development of charter schools accompanied by the narrative that they are the single best solution to the struggles in education. The Obama administration's Race to the Top initiative is heavily dependent on rapid charter school development. Charter schools run by EMOs use some public funding for their own employees, meaning that some of the public money not only is *not* going to the local schools, but also

does not stay in the community at all (Bracey 2002). Most EMOs seek out underprivileged communities in large part because of their immediate, acute needs,
an action that has the effect of further separating privileged schools from what
Darling-Hammond (2010) calls "apartheid schools" (p. 8). Broadly defined, charter schools are public schools (because they do not charge tuition) that are funded
by a combination of public and private sources. The private money means schools
are generally granted autonomy in curriculum development but must agree to
greater accountability. The "charter" of charter schools is a performance contract.
Because of the private funding and autonomous conditions, teachers generally are
not members of a union,[12] and teachers and administrative staff have no certification requirements (Buckley & Schneider 2007). That being said, the legislation
establishing charter schools has thus far has varied widely, and there are excep-
tions and alternatives to all these generalizations (Buckley & Schneider 2007).
Because of Obama's interest in charter schools, there may be increased clarity in
legislation, but part of their general appeal is that they remain independent and,
as a result, promise to increase competition between schools. Neoliberal arguments posit that competition will result in more strong schools and fewer weak
schools. The promise of charter schools has three main tenets: New schooling options for families in communities with few other options; increased connectivity
between schools and community businesses with an interest in education; and increased flexibility within the classroom. However, the reality of charter schools is
problematic: Maintaining high quality schools is extremely difficult, and charter
schools often operate in isolation from the larger community and other schools
(Payne & Knowles 2009).

There is no definitive evidence of the efficacy of charter schools. The breadth
of the literature illustrates a series of conflicting debates about all aspects of charter schools; some schools are extremely productive, while others are rife with
problems. Charter schools may–or may not–represent a war on public schools.
The promise of autonomy is not followed by a clear definition or application
of what, exactly, an autonomous school, staff or student body looks like. There
is no clear evidence that student achievement has increased or that students or
schools are being held to any greater standards of accountability. Charter schools
have, on average, a higher faculty attrition rate than traditional public schools.
Charter schools make many promises to students, teachers and families that are
both hard to keep and largely unsupported by evidence. One of charter schools'
biggest promises is to provide families with choice, but on closer examination,
this promise is complex. Before families are given "choice," a private organization
must determine that a struggling community is worthy of a new school. This
means that communities deemed too unattractive or too risky are passed over and
further dispossessed.[13] As painfully illustrated in Guggenheim's (2010) film *Wait-*

ing for "Superman," "choice" entails a debilitating lottery system based much more on blind luck than anything else.

When charter schools were first developed in the 1970s there was little to no interest in them. In the 1980s, with the release of the controversial *A Nation at Risk* report (National Commission 1983), government-funded research showed that American children were falling behind their peers in other countries, and there was increased interest in charter schools as a way to salvage what was believed to be faltering U.S. competitiveness against Cold War rivals (Bracey 2002). After the release of the "Contract with America," the 1994 Republican congressional manifesto detailing plans to overhaul education, among other things, interest in charter schools was reinvigorated (Wells 2002). Charter schools blossomed alongside conservative economic policy and increased faith in standardized testing as the measure of success. By the year 2000 there were between 1,700 and 2,000 charter schools, and by 2001 there were just under 2,400 charter schools in the United States (Bracey 2002; Wells 2002). At the turn to the 21st century there was slowed growth in charter school development, which Amy Wells (2002) attributes to "sheer exhaustion on the part of charter school founders and educators" (p. 1). The enthusiasm in *starting* a school is hard to sustain for *running* a school (Wells). Wells wrongly predicted "charter school reform is a late 20th century, laissez-faire reform that will die of its own weight some time early in the 21st century" (p. 2). With the Obama administration's faith in charter schools, they are once again on the rise.

Charter schools originally were intended not to compete with or overrun public schools but rather to function as small laboratories that would work to develop innovative solutions for problems in public education (Ravitch 2010). Within the free-market manifestation of schooling, charters now pluck the most promising students from struggling communities or, alternately, accept all students and then quietly encourage the lowest-achieving students back to their neighborhood schools (Ravitch 2010.) Charter school advocates argue that, free of bureaucratic restraint, creativity and learning will flourish, and charter schools will cure all of public education's ills (Bracey 2002). Charters divert funds from the public school system and bolster those monies with private funding, thereby weakening the public system. Charter schools accept fewer low-achieving students, including English-language learners, special education students and students with physical and mental disabilities and thus push these students further to the margins. Freedom from bureaucracy also means a murky relationship with transparency, especially in funding allocation and community eligibility (Bracey 2002). Overall, the promises made regarding autonomy and individuality have not extended to protecting the well-being of teachers or providing professional support (Wells 2002). Despite the absence of clarity, attention-grabbing charter schools also reduce crucial awareness of public schools.

Race to the Top

Like several presidents before him, Obama promised dramatic educational reform. It was not long before it became clear that his vision of education reform fell in lockstep with free-market principles and private industry (Brooks 2009). Obama allotted nearly $5 billion to education reform as part of the Race to the Top initiative. States and school districts were to compete for funding, starting with a lengthy, complex application process. In order to apply for funding, states were required to agree to develop common standards and assessments, to improve the effectiveness of teachers and principals, to develop and use data to inform decision making and to make a concerted effort to turn around the lowest performing schools.[14] The money allotted to Secretary of Education Arne Duncan "makes him the most powerful Secretary of Education ever" (Cruz 2009).[15] Just in order to apply, many states changed their policies or risked rejection. States with a cap on the number of charter schools, such as New York, were placed at a disadvantage to receive funds if they did not remove the cap (Fertig 2009). The application must describe multiple strategies for change and must have statements of support from leaders of local school districts, which in large states such as California could mean more than 1,000 letters (Dillon 2009b). Illinois, Louisiana and Tennessee raised caps on charter schools; every state except Texas and Alaska agreed to an initiative to develop common curricular standards for language arts and math; and California and Wisconsin allowed student achievement data to be used to evaluate teachers (Dillon 2010a; Rotella 2010). By February 2012, states that completed their applications or were in the midst of the requisite changes were eligible for NCLB waivers, alleviating pressure to meet the 2014 deadline of 100% math and reading proficiency (Hu 2012). These waivers effectively eliminated NCLB.

On the surface, the goals seem reasonable: Most people serious about education would agree that it is important to have clear curricular standards, that teachers and principals should be productive, that solid data improve research and that struggling schools should be improved. However, combing through the motivations of the reform initiative reveals a troublesome reality. States that did not adhere to the four goals were ineligible for funds, so the goal to increase competition was fulfilled before any money was dispersed. "Common standards and assessments" roughly translates to a national curriculum, a prospect that the history of American education reveals to be an unsavory, if not impossible, proposal (Ravitch 1983; Tienken & Canton 2009). Christopher Tienken and David Canton are against a national curriculum, writing that it "violates core principles of our democracy" and is an "educationally bankrupt" idea driven by "fears and political ideology" (p. 3). "Data informed decisions" invite surveillance of teachers, and "turning around low performing schools" translates to massive firings and school closings, where existing schools are replaced by EMO-run schools with nonunionized teachers. The most widespread criticism of Race to the Top is that there is little difference from No Child Left Behind (NCLB). Diane Ravitch, who once was in favor of charter schools but now is an outspoken critic of them, argues that the Race to the Top initiative is "in effect an extension of the Bush-era reforms" (qtd. in Cruz 2009). Ravitch (2010) found Obama's education plans "puzzling," writing, "here was a president who had been elected on a promise of change, yet he was picking up the same banner of choice, competition, and markets that had been the hallmark of his predecessors" (p. 146). With its emphasis on standardized testing, school accountability, performance pay and development of charter schools, Race to the Top is "little more than a dressed up version of the No Child Left Behind law" (Anderson 2009). This "dressing" is found in the language of student achievement. NCLB required that all students achieve proficiency in reading and math; Race to the Top requires that all students graduate from high school prepared for college and a career, which Sam Dillon (2010c) calls "equally elusive." Tienken and Canton caution that the Race to the Top money brings "strings attached to empirically fraudulent requirements such as linking teacher performance ratings and pay to student standardized test scores and creating more charter schools" (p. 5). One emphasis within school reform is greater attention to teachers, their role in the classroom and their impact on students.

Emphasis on teachers

In the *Harvard Education Review*'s 2009 special issue on the Obama presidency and education, essays include passionate pleas from schoolchildren to Obama to pay attention to their education, and especially to their teachers. Fifth grader Audrey Delgado writes, "The foundation, the glue, the peanut butter of the peanut butter and jelly sandwich, is the teacher.... If there aren't enough teachers, kids won't have a teacher to teach them. Isn't that the point of going to school?" (p. 226). The quality of the teacher makes a profound difference in student achievement, and yet teaching is not at present a top career choice for young adults.[16] Teachers are believed to be able to solve the crisis in education (Brown 2008; Ripley 2008). In order to entice people into teaching or encourage good teachers to do more, Race to the Top allots funds for merit and incentive pay. Erik Hanushek (2010) argues for the private business model of incentives and merit pay, writing, "The solution, of course, is to focus performance incentives for teachers and other school personnel on student achievement" (p. 95).

Merit and incentive pay entice teachers with financial rewards, following free-market principles without accounting for the hard work needed to develop a professionalized teaching corps. Darling-Hammond (2010) is an advocate for teacher professionalization, arguing for a plan that includes "universal high-quality teacher education; mentoring for all beginners; ongoing professional learning; leadership development; equitable, competitive salaries" (p. 198). Randi Weingarten (2010), the president of the American Federation of Teachers, also believes in the importance of outstanding teachers and is a firm supporter of teachers unions and a more holistic measurement of how to gauge teacher quality. Weingarten argues for five foundations of good teaching, including "good teachers supported by good leaders; good curricula; an environment that eliminates barriers to student success; shared responsibility and mutual accountabilities; collaboration, not competition or competitiveness" (p. 149). Weingarten makes the vitally important point that "teachers and students are not the only people involved in our nation's public education system" (p. 157) and that holding teachers accountable for all facets of student achievement is untenable. Good teachers can have a significant, positive impact on young people. Yet within the charter school model, teachers are inexperienced young professionals with little to no formal pedagogical training, hired by private industries. The systematic demonization of teachers and teachers unions means these new teachers work in an unprotected environment of fear and are trained to parrot private industry's ideas.

Popular Press Coverage of School Reform and School Reformers

In large part because most people have experienced both good and bad teachers and classrooms, many people feel entitled to an opinion of what would really, truly fix the problems in education. Whereas people might not feel qualified to make medical decisions without a medical degree, or policy decisions without a law degree, people do feel qualified to make pedagogical decisions without formal study of education. This is partly due to the variety of coverage provided by the popular press. The popular press does teach a great deal about education but needs careful analysis to better understand its role in the conversation.

In his analysis of the Edison Schools, Saltman (2005) observes that the popular press coverage of the company focused primarily on its role as a business, conspicuously ignoring its role in altering the face of education and thereby naturalizing and normalizing this role. He writes, "precious little of the press coverage explores in depth the implications for a democratic society of for-profit businesses running public schools" (p. 7). In his analysis of neoliberalism and disaster capitalism, Saltman (2007a) argues, "Mass media is one of the most powerful pedagogical forces continuously educating the public in understanding the economy as natural and inevitable" (p. 17). The mass media inform the public about multiple facets of education, often without critical analysis of larger implications. While the media continue to frame public conversations, there is little to no critique of their practice in large part because of a conspicuous absence in education of critical media literacy training. The popular press dutifully profiles major education reformers and reform movements in a way that naturalizes and normalizes the changes made with no critical analysis of the underlying neoliberal ethos.

Two of the most contentious figures in school reform, who receive a great deal of popular press coverage, are Secretary of Education Arne Duncan and former Washington, D.C. schools chancellor Michelle Rhee. Arguably the most nationally publicized school system–the one attended by the 20 participants studied in this text–is New York City's, the single largest public school system in the country, with more than one million students. The coverage of these individuals and this city is representative of how education is framed by the mainstream media, with an emphasis on aggressive, economically focused changes.

Much of the popular press coverage of Race to the Top focuses on Arne Duncan, who controls the greatest amount of money in modern history ever dedicated to school reform (Cruz 2009; Dillon 2009a). Prior to his appointment as Secretary of Education, Duncan was the CEO of Chicago public schools. Evidenced by his title–CEO–Duncan attempted to run the schools as a business. He worked to expand charter schools, pay students for good grades, provide merit pay for teachers and shut down failing schools, and he was noted for "his willingness to try anything, regardless of ideological association" (Cruz 2009). Yet this "willingness" did not produce success. Shutting down schools did not radically change many students' experiences "mainly because they ended up at schools that were as bad as the ones they had just left" (Cruz 2010). Duncan has no formal classroom teaching experience; he grew up in Chicago and spent afternoons at his mother's job, running an afterschool community center for underprivileged youth (Rotella 2010). As secretary of education, Duncan believes Americans can "educate ourselves out of a financial crisis" (qtd. in Rotella p. 25). In what appears to be a rare display of bipartisanship, Republicans otherwise disinterested in or hostile to Obama's policies "approve of Duncan's commitment to market-based reforms" (Rotella p. 25). This is, in fact, not a happy bridging of party politics but rather greater evidence that the Obama administration has more in common with free-market principles than with the progressive platform of socially and economically just change on which he campaigned. Giroux and Saltman (2008) lament that Duncan "does not have the slightest understanding of schools as something other than adjuncts of the corporation at best or the prison at worst."

Second in prominence to Duncan is former Washington, D.C. schools chancellor Michelle Rhee. Similar to how the media treated Duncan, they praise Rhee's radical aggressive actions despite her minimal classroom experience. After college, Rhee taught for three years before returning to graduate school and working in teacher recruitment (Brown 2008). She took over the Washington, D.C. school system in June 2007 with "no experience running a school, let alone a district with 46 thousand students that ranks last in math among 11 urban school systems" (Ripley 2008). Rhee was criticized for being young, not from Washington, D.C. and not African American (Ripley 2008) but not for her destructive choices. Rachel Brown (2008) praises Rhee's closing of 23 schools, restructuring

26 others and firing 46 principals as "accomplishments," representative of her "long-term emphasis on boosting teacher quality." Ripley (2008) praises Rhee for making "more changes than most school leaders," citing the school closings, teacher firings, streamlining of the Department of Education and, most radically, her removal of the principal of her daughters' elementary school, implying that she does not play favorites.

Both Duncan and Rhee are credited with unveiling what people do not like to see: The ugly reality of failing schools. With continuous press coverage, families (including those without children in public schools) are bullied into believing that without their support, a "reformer's particular style of quasi-missionary zeal could consign their kids to disaster" (Warner 2010, p. 11). In other words, "disaster" is emphasized to mask the reality that schools are not being healed but rather are being remade into the image of private industry.

Nowhere is this more evident than in New York City. The mayor-controlled school system receives much attention in large part because it is the single largest public school system in the nation, and home to some incredibly strong, vibrant schools, a series of poorly executed reform efforts and some profoundly challenged schools. For a number of years the schools were presided over by Superintendent Joel Klein, a business-oriented attorney with about six weeks of classroom experience. When Klein resigned at the end of 2010, the trajectory of the city's attention to school reform was made instantly clear by the choice of his replacement: Cathleen Black, the former chairwoman of Hearst Magazines. In a *New York Times* profile of her first days in office, as she visits several schools, Black is portrayed as uncomfortable in classrooms and unable to connect with children; indeed Black acknowledged that she had never before set foot in a New York City public school because both she and her children attended private schools (Dominus 2010). In April 2011, just four months into the position, Black resigned and was immediately replaced by Dennis M. Walcott, whose background was touted as being in line with the majority of the city's schoolchildren. Walcott is described by Fernando Santos (2011) in the *New York Times* as "a former teacher, with an easy rapport with children; a graduate of the city's public schools; 'a guy from Queens,' he said, whose parents were raised in Harlem and whose grandparents were immigrants." In this instance, a business leader–Black–was rejected, but in a school system controlled by a millionaire businessman, the business model prevails.

Readers are regularly reminded that Black, Rhee, Klein, Bloomberg and several other school leaders have little to no experience in classrooms. This invites a critique of the assumption that those with classroom experience automatically make good school leaders, and reinforces the promises of private industry's ability to streamline schooling. Despite Black's discomfort with classrooms and children, Susan Dominus (2010) writes, "maybe a steel will, an impenetrable façade and, yes, all that management experience will go further than any personal experience with hardship or previous service in the system." While it might not automatically follow that good teachers become good school leaders, the mass media construct an either/or division between teachers and business people: Either teachers or businesses will be in charge of schools, and thus far, teachers are not succeeding. Teachers with traditional education school training who join the union are demonized and labeled ineffective. Business is more radical and ruthless in its efforts. Rhee's public statements illustrate this divide. In a 2008 interview, she stated, "I think Joel Klein and [former Denver, Colorado Superintendent] Mike Bennet and Arne Duncan are some of the best superintendents around, and they were never teachers" (qtd. in Brown 2008). When Rhee (2010) resigned, she proclaimed, "The best way to keep the reform going in the D.C. schools was for me to leave my job as Chancellor." Rhee now runs an advocacy group called Students First that promotes vouchers for private schools, rates principals based on student achievement and works to abolish tenure (Banchero 2011).

The aggressive approach is played out in discussions of teacher performance, school choice and merit pay. The "grading" of teachers and principals on student performance and achievement puts pressure on teachers to make radical changes in little to no time with little to no professional development support, little to no security, and little to no flexibility. The assumption that business people can run schools further assumes that teachers can easily adopt a business ethos. Teachers with no business experience are expected to transfer their skills. Those who do are rewarded in the mainstream media. In March 2010 a Rhode Island school board fired the entire faculty of a poorly performing school, a move that President Obama publicly endorsed, causing "a storm of reaction nationwide, with teachers condemning it as an insult and conservatives hailing it as a watershed moment of school accountability" (Greenhouse & Dillon 2010). In 2007 the Baltimore County school board hired Andres Alonso to run the schools, and he "pushed through a sweeping reorganization of the school system, closing failing schools, slashing the central office staff by a third and replacing three-quarters of all school principals" (Tavernise 2010). The aggressive changes and provocative language–a "storm of reaction," "sweeping reorganization," closing, slashing, replacing–implies action and change. Change by whom, and with what intent–these questions are left unanswered. Alonso was not well liked by his colleagues or teachers, but in three years he got positive results, including decreased dropout rates, increased graduation rates and increased student enrollment. While this is laudable, it must be asked: How legitimate is this change? Otterman's (2011a) exploration of a Bronx, New York school showed that positive changes were falsified. Companies capitalizing on the disaster of public schools often make radical changes, and teachers and principals work in an environment of fear, tempered by promises for more pay. Baltimore teachers resigned themselves to Alonso's methods and are now "compensated based on performance" (Tavernise 2010). Teachers in KIPP schools work significantly longer hours than the average public school teacher and are compensated for their time but have zero job security (Mathews 2009). Teachers definitely deserve to be paid more, which makes merit pay seem like a good idea initially, but it operates as little more than a tactic to further push teaching towards a business model. Largely supported by the Obama administration, merit pay, "a once obscure free-market notion of handing cash bonuses to the best teachers, has lately become a litmus test for seriousness about improving schools" (Green 2010). Most well-known school reformers, including Klein, Duncan and Rhee all support merit pay for teachers, and Klein and Duncan have toyed with merit pay for students as well (Kohn 2008; Rhee 2010).

The mainstream media play a pivotal role in framing education change and development for the public. What is left unexplored is how the public experiences these changes, and what is left unheard is how young people who are schooled with these changes feel about and make meaning of their education. Do young people care about principal or teacher firings? Do they know how much their teachers are paid, or that their teacher will be paid more if they, the students, do well (and, alternately, that teachers might be fired if they, the students, do poorly)? Chapter Two starts to answer these questions by exploring where young people are and how they communicate; Chapters Three though Six draw directly from young people's stories to frame how they articulate their experiences with schooling. Chapter Seven argues further for an approach to pedagogy that includes critical media literacy as an intervention to neoliberalism.

"o i no its lazy of meee": Social Networking as Data Site

In May 2010 I moved out of New York City. This was a momentous change for me, fraught with struggle, yet grounded in excitement. On my last day as a New Yorker, I met with Popcorn to discuss my departure and how we would manage to continue our research together. In the two years since I had completed the research for *Media Education Goes to School*, I continued interviewing several participants as I plotted a long-term study of their transition out of high school. Although some of my participants had moved out of New York City, they came back often for family visits during semester breaks; it proved easy enough to conduct regular in-person and telephone interviews over the course of two years.

Popcorn had one solid idea for how we might continue our research without much struggle: If I would join Facebook, I could reconnect with "all" the Lincoln Square High School (LSHS) students, not just those with whom I was already in regular contact. He promised me that I would be found by all sorts of people right away and guaranteed they would be interested in continuing the research process electronically.

And so with much reluctance, I joined Facebook. I was not interested in living in the perpetual present tense, in having electronic "friends" or in leading such a public existence. And yet, according to the literature, that was exactly what young people wanted.[1] Admittedly, I was late to the Facebook platform and was completely unprepared for the response I got upon joining. Popcorn was right: Within just a few days, I was in touch with almost all my original participants and had "friended" and been "friended" by many former and current LSHS students. Every day, I received emails from Facebook letting me know that yet another young person wanted to be my friend; once I confirmed their friendships, these emails were followed by messages directly from the young people, generally along the lines of "wasssssss uppppp alllissssssonnnn!!!! I misssssss you!!" The exaggerated spelling and hyperbolic use of exclamation points unnerved me; part of my learning curve included tempering the written declaration of excitement as I found that my new electronic friends may have been sitting idly at their computers, with their smartphone or on their game consoles; despite the (apparent) excitement I became aware that my presence was merely a blip on their otherwise electronics-filled days (Roiphe 2010). The initial rush of messages and emails was intoxicating: Having just moved to a new town with no community connections, my quantity of electronic friends was comforting, if overwhelming.

Facebook, I was soon to learn, was a place of staggering (written) emotion and positive interpersonal connections. In very little time, seven of my original participants eagerly agreed to continue the long-term research electronically, and 13 new participants were excited to be a part of the process. My concerns about continuing interviews were set aside: I found that I learned a great deal about my participants by searching for them where they spent most of their time. Though I was unfamiliar–and, indeed, uncomfortable–on Facebook, I followed the guidelines of feminist qualitative research in order to make sense of the unfamiliar environment and learn what my participants were experiencing within their life changes and how they expressed themselves through their digital socializing.

Feminism, Postfeminism
and the Shifting Media Landscape

Qualitative research goes directly to the site; feminist qualitative research upends the site, tries to explore what is hidden, the unseen, an alternate perspective to the superficial presentation. Entering the research site through Facebook demands attention to shifts in media use, technology development and changes in socialization methods and means. Because Facebook has not been thoroughly explored as a site of data gathering, I rely on the methodology of feminist and critical cultural studies to best make sense of how to interrogate the digital environment.

In order to learn about the unfamiliar, I rely on the familiar. To best understand how young people make sense of change, I conducted in-person and electronic interviews and stayed closely connected to the site of research.[2] I create portraits of the participants based on my six-year knowledge of them as young people at a pivotal moment of transition and on their own constructions of self through their Facebook pages.[3] I map their stories, their participation on Facebook and the articulation of their life choices against feminist qualitative methods, analysis of the development and presentation of Facebook, and the current embodiment of education reform. There are distinct differences between young people's status updates, their day-to-day lives and the ways in which they participate in a semi-formal interview; these differences need to be carefully explored not to rationalize, defend or celebrate what young people do online and in their mundane worlds but to better understand how they construct their digital selves, what they understand about "public" and "private" information and how the digital realm is no less real to them than the tangible world.

Feminism works as an interruption,[4] asking scholars and activists to put what they think they know on hold and reexamine the field from an alternate perspective. Feminism asks scholars to move beyond their own comfortable positions and work to better understand an articulation of the "other." While the adult scholar can never truly appropriate the identity project of young people, it is his/her responsibility to explore, most fully, how that project develops. Angela McRobbie (2008) challenges feminist scholars to regularly re-examine the inquiry process; this often entails looking beyond one's own experiences and comforts. As a feminist critical cultural studies scholar invested in qualitative methods, I was comfortable with interviewing and observing young people; I was, however, quite resistant to participating in social networking. I allowed my absence of understanding and my own discomfort to limit my awareness and understanding of young people. By stepping through that discomfort and joining them in their familiar space, I learned more about this group of young people and their current social and political positioning than I could have from observing and engaging them in a strictly physical space; to ignore or bypass the digital will limit knowledge development. In visiting young people in their familiar space, I was able to learn how they projected themselves, their struggles at moments of monumental change and the ways in which they made the digital space a safe and productive environment. I learned what they valued in self-presentation and how they expressed their concerns and joys about interpersonal relationships, academic and work experiences and personal development. By exploring their words, updates and life experiences, I was able to learn about how they saw themselves as burgeoning adults. This book opens with the claim that the foundations of critical cultural studies remain important for understanding contemporary postmillennial youth, and I believe the application of feminist cultural studies to the study of young people helps us understand the political shifts of youth cultures, media, technology and education.

Now is the time when a further interruption is needed in feminist cultural studies in order to make sense of 21st century studies of youth, technology and education. This is where the tropes of postfeminism can be helpful. Postfeminism, which emerged in the 1990s, takes on the Western perspective that the personal and the popular are intimately fused (Siegel 2007; Tasker & Negra 2007; Zaslow

2009). Postfeminist theory acknowledges the political gains made by the now-traditional, seemingly centrist feminism of the 1960s to 1970s but sees those battles as both complete and in no danger of returning (McRobbie 2007). Today, both male and female youth grow up in an environment of conflicting messages. One prevalent message constructed within postfeminism tells them they can do it all, that girls are as capable as boys of addressing any challenge. However, under-lying the ideology of being able to "do it all" is a conspicuous absence of educa-tion or social services supporting young people in their endeavors and minimal attention to how young people feel about these messages. There is little clarity of what "it all" means, and paths to success are murky at best, especially in times of economic crisis. Traditional routes to success are no longer necessarily viable and what constitutes "success" is framed as personal and individual. Postfeminist theory holds that youth of secure socioeconomic status with an above-adequate education have access to "it all," while urban youth of color from struggling so-cioeconomic backgrounds with subpar educational experiences have a difficult fight to access "it all." Yet, because of widely accessible popular media and because advances in technology make media more mobile and significantly less expensive, socioeconomically struggling young people are invited *partially* into the celebra-tion that marks postfeminism: They are invited to witness but not participate fully in the celebration of individual achievement.

In this way, postfeminism is fused with neoliberalism and the ideas of market freedom, personal choice and responsibility. Both postfeminism and neoliberal-ism teach young people that they have unlimited choices and that success or failure is their personal responsibility. Both postfeminism and neoliberalism teach the larger population that all digital, technological and political desires are best realized through the free market. Both postfeminism and neoliberalism are inti-mately connected to advances in technology, especially mobile and digital media and social networking. Increased access to advanced technologies gives the im-pression that the individual user has greater control over his/her participation as audience or creator.

Scholars and critics have diverse views on the myth or promise of the Inter-net. Evgeny Morozov (2011), a technological celebrationist and political skeptic, believes the Internet has great promise but risks succumbing to antidemocratic authoritarian control. With a focus on concerns for security and privacy, he cau-tions against Internet-centrism that focuses "only on the intrinsic qualities of on-line tools at the expense of studying how these qualities are mitigated by the contexts in which the tools are used" (p. 148). Lee Siegel (2008), a technological skeptic, cautions against celebrating the Internet, calling it, at best, "a marvel of convenience" (p. 3). Sherry Turkle (2011) combines technological analysis with psychological analysis to argue that advanced digital communication technologies shift who we are as people and as communicators. She writes, "our new devices provide space for the emergence of a new state of the self, itself split between the screen and the physical real, wired into existence through technology" (p. 16). Social networking has been credited with both promoting and limiting activism because the digital environment invites a seemingly infinite number of people to become involved, but it remains unclear *how* people define "involvement." Malcolm Gladwell (2010) argues social networking does *not* revolutionize activism, rather, it enables the tools and convenience of activism. In contrast, Jose Vargas (2011) and Ned Parker (2011) believe the Internet and social networking have exponentially increased democratic participation.

The ease and convenience of digital mobile media raise questions of audience role and responsibility. New media and the Internet are not inherently democratic, though through the lens of neoliberalism, they certainly present themselves as such. The rise of, and advances in, digital mobile media invites increased citizen participation as well as increased corporate media control (Newman & Scott 2005). The promise of the Internet for some was that it would usher in a renewed commitment to democratic media. Unfortunately, corporate control and the free market grew in lockstep with the Internet. In his continued advocacy for the free press, Robert McChesney (2005) writes, "in 'free market' mythology, our media system is the result of competition between businesses fighting to best meet public needs. In reality, civic needs aren't even on the radar" (p. 11). What is believed to be "free," particularly the Internet, is anything but. The myth of the Internet, he argues, is that citizens need not worry "about corrupt policymaking, corporate control, lousy journalism, or hypercommercialism" because when broadcast scarcity is replaced with Internet abundance, all citizens have equal access (p. 17). McChesney cautions that "merely having the ability to launch a website does not magically transform the media system" (p. 17). Just because citizens are present and active does not automatically shift the environment; rather, it provides the illusion of change.

The democracy thought to be inherent in digital technology is elusive. Because of supposed digital democracy, Turkle (2011) notes, people are left to make up their own rules, and it becomes increasingly difficult to "turn off" our communication with others. Siegel (2008) laments, "we start to behave in public as if we were acting in private, and we begin to fill our private world with gargantuan public appetites" (p. 18). Most insidious, however, is that mobile, digital content and technologies infiltrate and become intricately woven into our everyday activities.

Facebook and Qualitative Methods Collide

Qualitative research strives for as "natural" an environment as possible in order to best know and make sense of participants in their worlds. In the space of Facebook I could "hear" how the participants expressed themselves both in the interview situation and in their daily digital activities. Conducting research via Facebook allowed me to interview participants while observing them in an environment they consider natural. Multiple scholars of technology and youth posit that today young people grow up with the expectation of continuous connection; young people grow up with Facebook as a wholly familiar presence.[5] In learning about the participants through social networking, I was able to see the ways in which they frame themselves and desire to be seen. I witnessed the interpersonal connections and squabbles, conflicts and resolutions. If I log on to Facebook regularly, I am able to consistently enter the field and can regularly observe their developments in a quasi-anthropological exploration (Geertz 1983). Entry to and disengagement from the field is not an arduous separation from my own daily life, and yet, the field is a different space in many important ways. Facebook is a potentially powerful setting for ethnographic data gathering. Having known the participants since 2006, I was able to see their growth and better understand the context of their changes.

Facebook is not a flawless research site; it does not eliminate the challenges and struggles of qualitative data gathering. There is precious little scholarly research about Facebook, and it has not been thoroughly studied as a data-gathering site. Most research on social networking focuses on how it is used by young people; how adults, especially teachers, use it to better connect with students; and its integral role in digital and technological development.[6] The ease of participant acquisition and the joy of reconnecting with vital, vivacious young people were confounded by challenges inherent to digital communication: Lack of context, body language cues and linguistic techniques and a different way of knowing people. I could use Facebook as a research site only because I knew and had established tangible relationships with the participants. Our prior knowledge of each other—a close working rapport and, for seven participants, previous experience working with me in research—facilitated the process. The colloquialisms and body language found in in-person interviews are harder to translate through Facebook. Many young people connect to Facebook via their smartphones and therefore, make much use of complex shorthand, abbreviations and creative spelling. The role of researcher and participant is shifted, particularly when the participants are more familiar with the digital environment than the researcher. At the early stages, I relied heavily on participants to explain much of their digital shorthand and I spent a lot of time deciphering the abbreviations. Entering Facebook is similar to learning a foreign language, albeit one that can only be read, not spoken. Much of what I thought I knew about young people was upended when they were examined through a completely new (to me) frame. Conducting research via Facebook invites a facilitation approach to the research, adhering to the tenets of critical media literacy where the researcher is not the primary source of knowledge (Buckingham 2003). It is admittedly unnerving to be uncomfortable in an environment so natural to young people, but embracing that discomfort yields productive, rich results.

There are vast differences between interview answers and the status updates posted by the majority of the participants; the interview responses are clearly filtered in a different way than status updates. I think neither of these are "lies" (or, for that matter, the only "truth"), rather they are context-specific responses and part of the performance of Facebook (Turkle 2011). As an adult conducting research, albeit one the participants have known for many years, interviews are inherently more formal than status updates. I am the primary recipient of interview data and the only one who knows the "true" identity of participants; I organize and analyze interview data through formal processes, while status updates are less protected, and shared with potentially countless recipients. The researcher's responsibility is to make sense of the distinctions and pay close attention to context. I believe the participants took the written interview questions seriously[7] and provided thorough, complex answers, but they rarely checked their spelling or grammar. In-person audio/video interviews may be colloquial and filled with slang, but the primary investigator/transcriber is responsible for translating the spoken to the written word. Should written interviews be cleaned up or are the colloquial misspellings part of the context?

To unpack this question, consider a moment from the interview process with one participant. Serenity, a young African American woman, submitted long, thoughtful (if misspelled and colloquially written) answers to interview questions. She regularly posts her observations on humanity, boys, personal responsibility, gender politics, family roles, work and school updates to Facebook. I have known Serenity, currently a senior in college, since she was in high school in New York City. She and her twin brother were raised in a series of foster homes after the death of their mother. Though their grandparents were still alive, they were too elderly to care for small children. As teenagers, Serenity and her brother were placed under the legal guardianship of their deceased mother's best friend. Serenity was a member of the first graduating class of LSHS and initially attended a private college in the South on an academic scholarship. She had no family or friends near her school, and, frustrated, she transferred to a public college just outside of Baltimore, Maryland, where she has extended family members. She holds two jobs, attends classes full time and maintains an "A" average. Serenity is a bright, capable, independent young woman. She also succumbs to the ease and laziness afforded by Facebook. Within minutes of submitting her answers to a set of primary interview questions, she popped up on the chat function and wrote me the following:

> kay,i type from my phone so have typos,plz excuse me,i dont normally write so jacked up,its just facebook i dont feel like proofreading sometimes. im serious,if

its not a paper for school or sumthing i really need to proofread, i wontttt, o i no
its lazy of meee,ima start doing betta soon as i get energy lol.

In the space of Facebook, this language is not only accepted, it is expected. As a
written document, Serenity's message is undoubtedly a mess, but reading it as a
casual, spoken conversation allows one to see how she processes her emotions,
what she takes seriously and what knowledge she has of her own culpability in
this situation.

For the sake of clarity and ease of reading, I have cleaned up the writing by
participants: I have fixed their spelling and, on some occasions, have made formal some colloquialisms. Any colloquialisms remaining are assumed common
parlance or explained more thoroughly in the text. While I concede that some
personal meanings or intentions might be slightly altered, I worked to translate
their words most responsibly and gave participants the opportunity to respond
if desired. When appropriate, I describe and share their online activities, but not
so explicitly as to give away their identities. All participants chose their own code
names, and while I share some of their Facebook patterns and quote them at
length, I do so from private communication. No identifying information from
their Facebook profiles is revealed.

The Changing Face of the Digital Environment

Facebook has more than 750 million active users, with the United States contributing about 30% of global users (Facebook.com 2011, *Statistics*).[8] Facebook is an
extraordinarily popular social networking site, especially with young people, who
are the most prolific users of digital media and the Internet. Social networking
sites are to the 21st century what the mall was to (suburban) teens in the late 20th
century and dance halls were to the teens of the mid-20th century: the place to
congregate (boyd 2009). In her study of MySpace, danah boyd (2007b) writes that
social networking sites "developed significant cultural resonance amongst American teens in a short period of time" (p. 1). From about 2003 to 2005, MySpace
was the social network site where teens congregated, and it was especially friendly
for the advertising and marketing of independent musicians and artists. However,
with MySpace's buyout by News Corp in 2005 and Facebook's opening in 2006
to a broader audience beyond Harvard University students, the field shifted. For a
brief period, Sconex, a social networking site designed specifically for high school
students, was popular, but the appeal of MySpace and the allure of Facebook won
out and Sconex[9] was shut down (Anastasia 2008).

Young people spend a great deal of time online, especially on Facebook, posting near-constant newsfeed updates and creating a platform to introduce their
presence on other media sites. The third wave of the Kaiser Family Foundation's

study of young people's media usage, which pays particular attention to the rapid rise, possession and use of mobile, digital technology and the increase of media multitasking by young people, observes that two of the most popular computer-related activities–social networking and YouTube–"barely existed five years ago" (Rideout, Foehr & Roberts 2010, p. 21). In her 2006–2007 study of self-presentation and social networking, Zeynep Tufekci (2008) found that just over 85% of her sample had at least one social network profile, "a particularly striking fact since these sites have existed in their current format for only a few years" (pp. 25–26). Facebook is firmly entrenched in a digital environment that teaches its users that multitasking is a normal activity. According to the Pew Internet and American Life Project, teenagers and those in their twenties and early thirties "are the most likely groups to use the Internet for entertainment and for communicating with friends and family" (Jones & Fox 2009, p. 7). "Entertainment" includes online videos, online games and downloaded music. Young people multitask their media activities and pack just under 11 hours of media content into 7½ hours of usage, "an increase of almost 2¼ hours of media exposure per day over the past five years" (Rideout, Foehr & Roberts, p. 2). By the beginning of the 21st century, college students used the Internet for help with schoolwork, to interact with professors and especially for socializing (Jones 2002). Digital mobile media do not just enhance but are intimately part of young people's social lives. The transition from high school to college changes when it is easy for young people to maintain long-term childhood relationships through technology. In the face of challenging and unfamiliar environments, the ties maintained through digital technology can be a vital source of support (Jones 2002; Steinfield, Ellison & Lampe 2008). Post-high school and college students use social networking, and Facebook in particular, in part to maintain secure connections with long-term friends.

Increased mobile technology and easy access to online media, especially increased content available online as well as social networking, contribute to young people's increased multiple media use. Visiting Facebook is the most popular computer activity for 8– to 18–year-olds (Rideout, Foehr & Roberts 2010). While Internet and digital media use increases, email use has decreased for young people. In 2004, 89% of teens claimed to use email; this number dropped to 73% by 2009 (Jones & Fox 2009). According to Turkle (2011), email is considered "a technology of the past, perhaps required to apply to college or to submit a job application" (p. 162). Email is considered a burdensome waste of time when most young people communicate via messaging or chatting on Facebook. Young people do not appear bothered by–or even aware of–the multiple demands made on their time by media multitasking. Turkle comments, "When I ask teenagers specifically about being interrupted during homework time, for example, by Facebook messages or new texts, many seem not to understand the question. They say things like, 'That's just how it is. That's just my life'" (p. 163).

Harvard University student Mark Zuckerberg started Facebook in February 2004 as a digital connection for Harvard students. It quickly became a place for more university students to connect digitally when, within the year, Zuckerberg and his early partners/classmates Dustin Moskovitz, Chris Hughes and Eduardo Saverin opened the site to three other Ivy League schools, Stanford, Columbia and Yale. By 2005 the site was opened up to all American university students with an .edu address, and later to all individuals around the globe, regardless of email address or location.[10]

While Facebook (and Zuckerberg in particular, who publicly and contentiously broke ties with his original collaborators) is credited with remaining "independent" of corporate media control, it is not wholly independent. In 2008 Zuckerberg hired Sheryl Sandberg from Google to be Facebook's chief operating officer and within two years, Facebook began turning a healthy profit (Auletta 2011). Sandberg has kept Facebook "free" to users, making money instead from advertising applications that are creative both in how the advertisements appear (in the margins) and in their use of suggestions based on what users' friends like. 2011 rumors that Facebook would soon go public (Auletta) were confirmed in early 2012 (Raice 2012). Though Zuckerberg turned down offers of purchase from MTV Networks, Yahoo! and Microsoft, he has not turned away from strategic partnership opportunities (Vargas 2010). The company stood firm behind the language of "strategic partnerships" with corporate stockholders, Microsoft to develop banner advertisements, CNN for live feeds and most recently, Skype to enable video chatting.[11] Strategic partnerships such as these are a concern of Russell Newman and Ben Scott (2005) and McChesney (2005), who see them and their ilk as a dangerous portent for increased corporate control. Corporations have long infiltrated social networking sites by creating profiles as extensions of their brand identity. Corporations do not need to own social network outlets as long as they can have a highly visible presence *within* them. Facebook integrates its desire for profit and control of the social networking model seamlessly into its layout. The "like" button, introduced in 2009, invites friends to like each others' status updates and photographs, while also inviting individuals to like public pages devoted to products and celebrities. In this way, Facebook archives all the links and likes of its users; when users like something or someone, they are in fact working (for free) for Facebook's advertising and marketing department, a process eerily reminiscent of that detailed in Smythe's (1981) analysis of television viewing.

Despite its broad range of users, Facebook still reveals the tropes of its Ivy League start-up: all Facebook pages and, by extension, Facebook users, succumb to the carefully constructed, seamless look of the site. While users can upload as many photos as they want, name themselves whatever they want, post as many links as they want, and, ostensibly, create as many pages as they want, all this is done within a blue and white organizational scheme that clearly divides the page into tidy compartments. Despite any one individual's personal touches, all Face-book pages are framed exactly the same. Status updates, commentary and con-versations all occur within the middle of the page. The left side of the home page shows the user's information, including how many of his/her friends are online. The right side of the page shares links the user might find helpful and nudges the user towards these links with proclamations of which friends found those links helpful. This margin also consistently encourages the user to find more friends through posting links to friends of friends. Sometimes friends' photos are posted in this margin, and there are always links to businesses that might be of interest, based on the user's geographic location or travel interests, gender and ethnicity.

Facebook represents a valuable site for exploring contemporary identity poli-tics. Exploring young people through Facebook and using it as the interview site tend to undo the tradition of seeing young people as "problems."[12] The digital revolution as experienced by young people asks scholars to re-explore important questions of race/ethnicity, class, gender, sexual identity and socializing as part of the identity development project. While Facebook users are roughly evenly divided between male and female, Facebook use is not gender neutral. Sheila Cot-ton, William Anderson and Zeynep Tufekci (2009) argue that digital technologies and social networking represent a new division of gender, between social affirma-tion (feminine) and play (masculine). Walther et al. (2008) look particularly at the connections between quantity of friends and perceived attractiveness. They found that posting onto Facebook unattractive images of men who appeared to have had too much to drink the night before raised the men's desirability, whereas similar images of women decreased the women's desirability. A corresponding study found that "individuals who have too few friends or too many friends are perceived more negatively than those who have an optimally large number of friends" (Tong, Van Der Heide, Langwell & Walther 2008, p. 545). The "cor-rect" amount of friends is not a strict number but rather a perception of what is appropriate. According to Facebook, the average user has 130 friends (Facebook. com 2011, *Statistics*). The participants in my study had anywhere from just over 100 to just under 1,000 friends.

At this point in the development of scholarship, there is no singular narrative of social networking sites, and there are key contradictions that need to be worked through. boyd (2007b) argues that accounting for race/ethnicity and social class presents no variation in use by young people while Mary Celeste Kearney (2006) finds that race and gender do have an impact on usage. There appears to be an increase in both access to social networking and use by young people of color (Kearney 2006; Vargas 2009), but no clear narrative on who is using which tech-nology for what purpose. According to the Kaiser Family Foundation (Rideout, Foehr & Roberts 2010), Latino and African American youth "average about 13 hours of media exposure daily, compared to just over 8½ hours among whites"

(p. 5). The assumption that the increased presence of young people online means they are more digitally recognizable is critiqued by Lynn Schofield-Clark's (2008) observation that young people can "'hide' behind the computer to afford themselves more security in social situations they perceive as risky" (p. 216). The work young people do within the larger realm of social networking might not make sense to an outside (adult) observer, but as boyd (2009) explains, the "completely irrational, or pointless at best" conversations are "a form of social grooming" (p. 5). Concerns about Internet predators, cyberbullying and inappropriate behavior by children and teens are countered by qualified rationalizations that young people generally "friend" people they know in "real life," that behavior in Facebook is not so different from pre-digital adolescent angst and experimentation and that media reports of digital criminal behavior, while frightening, are wildly exaggerated because they are more enticing than reports on the banal use by most young people.[13] What is agreed is that digital media and social networking shift the understanding and application of technology, and young people play a particularly salient role.

There seem to be innumerable Facebook pages that one can like. Users can like pages or groups, and a series of random phrases entered into the search bar will show how many other people have similar random likes or thoughts. There is no corresponding "dislike" button, so anything deemed offensive or problematic must be handled differently than that which is approved or enjoyed. Likes are archived as part of Facebook's advertising and marketing scheme, while "dislikes" serve as commentary. If a link to something that is deemed problematic or offensive to the user and his/her friends is shared, it is archived, so even disliked material has a click count. The only way, it seems, to truly dislike something is to ignore it entirely.

Any changes made to a user's page are updated in the newsfeed and status update section and accompanied by the user's profile picture. The default privacy setting is absolutely no privacy at all: Anyone at any time can see any part of a user's page unless the user him/herself manipulates what is shared or restricted. One of the most oft-repeated complaints and concerns about Facebook is the absence of privacy, especially when the system makes changes or updates the platform, thereby altering "everyone's" privacy settings.[14] All updates are time- and date-stamped and may appear chronologically or as what Facebook determines to be "top news" (updates with the most commentary or from a particularly popular site). How a user posts status updates–whether the posting is from a smartphone or video game console, for example–and from where, geographically, is specifically noted. The more specific a user is about his/her interests and the more a user posts and/ or comments, the more particularly tailored the page's right margin becomes. An estimated 50% of users sign on every day and users spend over 700 billion minutes per month on the site (Facebook.com 2011, *Statistics*). Users interact with

900 million items, including pages, groups, events and community pages and the average user is connected to 80 pages, groups, events and community pages (Facebook.com 2011, *Statistics*).

Zuckerberg wants to shift the way information is organized, from an index format to a holistically shared and mutually influential format. This shift, if successful, means that, once again, users will tacitly agree to give up more personal information. Zuckerberg's goal is to have users engage in all social activities with Facebook as a participant (Auletta 2011; Vargas 2010), which means an increased erosion of privacy. The more postings on Facebook, the greater the network connections, and the larger one's digital footprint becomes. Despite some concerns with privacy, the general feeling appears to be an increased acceptance of sharing a variety of information (Miller 2010). Though users sometimes become angry that Facebook collects more personal information than any other company and regularly manipulates privacy settings, Auletta (2011) observes that the cycle of anger already follows a familiar pattern. Commenting on the inclusion of facial recognition software that automatically identifies all participants in a photograph, he writes, "users complained, Facebook apologized, and the program was modified but not eliminated" (p. 62). What remains unknown is how long Facebook can monopolize this data.[15]

A continued debate within the realm of Facebook, particularly for those concerned with young people, is who we are on Facebook. Few illusions are harbored that our "true" selves are presented in a singular narrative or that Facebook is not a carefully orchestrated performance (Miller 2010; Roiphe 2010). Turkle (2011) argues, "we use social networking to be 'ourselves,' but our online performances take on lives of their own" (p. 160). Facebook becomes a performance site but, breaking from Erving Goffman (1959), it blurs front and back regions. As Turkle notes, "when one has time to write, edit and delete, there is room for performance. The 'real me' turns out to be elusive" (p. 180). Facebook teaches us to expect the performance. As Siegel (2008) observes, "people have now come to expect inner life to be performed, rather than disclosed. The truth or untruth of facts presented as facts in the course of a performance is never at issue" (p. 51). The "real me" on Facebook goes through many interpersonal challenges, often starting with who qualifies as "friend." Turkle (2011) details the multiple incarnations of "friend" on Facebook, including how to balance public and private information. Tufekci (2008) writes that her college-aged participants "*do* try to manage the boundary between publicity and privacy, but they do not do this by total withdrawal because they would then forfeit a chance for publicity" (p. 33, italics in original). According to Ross et al. (2009), because young people mostly friend people they already know from the offline world, "it does not appear that Facebook users are primarily concerned with privacy" (p. 579). As a performance site for its users, Facebook invites a level of play whose boundaries are malleable.

Electronic Interviews and Participant Observation

I make no effort to generalize the participants' experiences to the larger population of young adults or Facebook users. Schofield-Clark's (2008) study of girls'
experiences with technology employs the rationale that in-depth interviewing
"grows out of a desire to begin the study with attention to how young people
themselves explain what is important to them about their new media use" (p.
208). Vargas (2009) employs action research as a "process-oriented methodology that pursues understanding as well as social justice" (pp. 6–7). The stories
of the participants are shared to show how they make sense of their life changes.
Scholars of youth, the media and education may make more nuanced use of social
networking to better understand young people and their experiences. Using Facebook as a data-gathering site, this research explores how these young people make
sense of their growth and of pivotal life changes. With respect to social justice, I
aim to use the participants' stories to support more thoroughly nuanced changes
in public education, including an immersion of critical media literacy, in order to
make schools more productive for all students, irrespective of their socioeconomic
backgrounds.

I first met the participants in 2006 when I worked to develop the media education curriculum at LSHS in New York City. The students who attended LSHS
were part of Mayor Bloomberg's takeover of the public school system. Starting in
2002, he began closing large comprehensive high schools and replacing them with
small, theme-based schools in the belief that small schools and small classrooms,
organized around a particular idea or guiding force would be pedagogically beneficial to at-risk, underserved youth (Ancess & Allen 2006; Butler 2010). Seven
of the current participants were also a part of my research on how young people
make meaning of media education within their urban school (Butler 2010) and
have continued work with me over the years.[16]

This research has developed over the course of four years, following the
growth and development of 20 participants as they move out of high school and
into college and work environments. The participants graduated from high school
between 2008 and 2010. One participant dropped out of LSHS because of an
overwhelming number of interpersonal and disciplinary problems, then enrolled
in another school a year later for a traditional high school diploma. The participants range in age from 18 to 21, are evenly distributed by gender and represent a
range of race/ethnic backgrounds: Nine self-identify as Latino/a, eight as African
American, two as Asian, and one as white. Ten of the participants graduated from
high school in 2008, five in 2009 and five in 2010. Twelve of the participants
currently attend college and seven of those 12 transferred to other schools after
their first or second year. Four of the 12 attend private colleges; seven attend local
community colleges in New York City and one attends a public university outside

the city. Three participants want to attend college once they resolve financial difficulties. One participant plans to join the Marines, but in the years since he left high school he still has not signed up. The participants who do not attend college work a series of part-time jobs.

Why Do These Young People Use Facebook?

All of the participants are regular, consistent users of Facebook. Their quantity of listed friends varies from just over 100 to just under 1,000, with the average at just over 400. Three of the participants hide their friends list, while most acknowledge they have done nothing to alter their privacy settings. Some, such as Serenity, post regularly; others post more rarely. Without regular posting, it can be hard to tell how often young people sign on. Many of them started their social networking experience with a MySpace or Sconex page, but as they grew older, MySpace waned in popularity and Sconex closed–it was never very appealing for young people who aspired to the perceived sophistication of MySpace or Facebook. For the most part, the participants use Facebook to keep in touch with real-life friends, especially as they or their friends move out of the close confines of high school and possibly beyond New York City. Brick, a young white man who graduated from high school in 2010 and attends a private college north of New York City, explains:

> To tell you the truth, I really don't know. I guess I use Facebook because it is a way of keeping in contact with people. It lets me see how my other friends are doing even though the friends I do care about I can just text or call for the most part. So, I guess it's to keep in contact with those I don't have phone numbers for or really talk to outside of Facebook.

That Brick starts off with "I don't know" reveals how intertwined Facebook is in his life: It is something that is there and seemingly always has been. Through his exploration of friendship–keeping in contact, to see how others are doing and to keep in touch with peripheral friends–the types of "Facebook friends" are clear.

Bruce is a young African American man who lives in Brooklyn, New York and graduated from high school in 2008. He sporadically attends a local community college in Brooklyn. He emphasizes the convenience of Facebook:

> I use FB to keep up with peers. People will write me on this site before they text me, even family. Both my older siblings have group-messaged people in the family to plan trips and family gatherings. And FB is just a convenient way to keep up with individuals with pictures, statuses, etc.

Bruce echoes Turkle's (2011) discussion that young people find email cumbersome: They can take care of "all" communication via Facebook. Facebook's convenience is echoed by many of the participants:

> *John:* I use Facebook because it allows for the connection and interaction of friends and family when one cannot interact in person or wants to interact and exchange ideas with many friends.

> *Serenity:* I use Facebook as a way to keep updated with friends and family and say what's on my mind.

> *Natalie:* I use Facebook as a means of communication with friends and long distance family. It helps me keep in contact with some old teachers as well. I check Facebook very often. It also lets me know gossip and what everyone else is up to. I think many people use Facebook as a way to let people know how or what they're doing with their life. Facebook became a big thing to me after high school. I lost contact with many people and this is how I regained some of it.

> *Nino:* I used to have MySpace. And I used to have Sconex. I deleted my Sconex to get MySpace. Then I deleted my MySpace to get Facebook. And I just did it 'cause a lot of my friends from high school and a lot of family are on it, it's a good way to keep in touch. You can share videos and photos and status updates. I don't like to make mine really that personal. I know some people write their whole life on in and I don't understand why. I just think it's crazy to put your whole life on Facebook. I like using it to share my experiences with old friends or new people. I can keep in touch, they're like "Oh, what you doing? You need to come visit me!" It reminds me of high school. You know, all those fun conversations I used to have and it's a good way for family members to like see photos of me and my brother and the rest of the family.

Nino, a young Latina who graduated from high school in 2008, keeps in touch with friends she met when she lived in California for a year. She explained that they messaged her and posted to her wall in winter months that she should escape the cold of New York City to visit them in sunny, warm California. John, a young Latino who graduated from high school in 2010 and wants to attend college, currently works in his uncle's bodega and babysits his two nieces. He is afraid to apply to college because he and several family members are in the country illegally and he does not want to get caught. He posts quite frequently on Facebook, often commenting on television shows while he watches them, and provides links to mainstream news coverage of current events. He is a passionate young man, and Facebook is an outlet for him to share what he feels is important without feeling ostracized as he did in high school, when his fellow classmates did not express as much interest in current events as he did. Serenity, whose impassioned plea to trust her ability to proofread was the inspiration for this chapter, also posts quite frequently. Her posts tend to be about the frustrations or joys of one of her multiple part-time jobs as well as commentary on how school is going and what she expects out of a man when she feels ready to settle down. Natalie, a young Latina who lives in Brooklyn and attends community college in Manhattan is sporadic in her postings. She explained to me that she tends to post more when she is stressed and that she uses Facebook to maintain contact with people from a time when she felt more secure.

Not all participants are regular Facebook users; some are rare posters who use the site to keep in touch with people. Jacline, a young Latina who graduated from high school in 2008, attended a private college in upstate New York before becoming ill and returning to the city to attend a public college. She explains:

> I almost never get on. I sign in and check my email maybe once a week and get right back out. I get on Facebook because I know that it's where I can find everyone in one place and where I can talk with people I've known throughout my life. I barely get on, but when I do it's to get in contact with someone or to see who got in contact with me.

Technically, Jacline cannot check her email via Facebook; she can check her messages, but those are only accessible by signing onto the site, thereby making her presence known.

Some of the participants profess to use Facebook for a combination of personal and professional reasons:

> *Peter:* Facebook is not a necessary aspect of my life, simply put. I don't need it. I reactivated it because of complaints from friends asking me to come back and for business purposes (networking mainly). So I use it to network and to help friends keep in touch with me.

> *Planet J:* I use Facebook to connect with friends, to make new friends, and to keep updated with the progress of everyone within my network. I also use Facebook to advertise myself. I do not use it as a professional outlet, but I do use it to contact other people professionally.

> *Stacey:* I go on Facebook to either put new pictures up, be nosy or when I am bored and do not want to do my work. But I mainly use it for my e-board position as PR manager on our NAACP chapter to promote events on campus to our peers.

Peter, a young African American man who graduated from high school in 2008, attended a local community college in Brooklyn for a year before getting a scholarship to a traditional black college in the South. Unfortunately, he could not keep up with the workload and was put on academic suspension; he returned for a semester to New York City and attended community college. Working diligently and finding the focus and determination needed for the private university, he has since returned to the South and is doing well. Though he claims he does not need Facebook, he does post regularly, especially when school ends for the semester. Planet J is a young African American man who graduated from high school in 2008 and attends community college in Queens, New York. He and his best friend are aspiring filmmakers and they often post their work to Facebook. Stacey is a young African American woman who graduated from high school in 2009; she attends a private university on Long Island where she is involved in many student organizations. Through Facebook, these three participants practice networking; they regularly post silly updates, pictures from social activities, or comment on the stress of school. They also see the site as a place where they can practice professional skills they believe they will need in the future.

For the most part, the participants do not question their use of Facebook; it is a part of their lives and a primary form of communication. As Brick stated, he does not even know why he uses Facebook—it is just consistently available. Akin to Turkle's (2011) findings, they take for granted their ability to communicate constantly. In May 2010, when Popcorn convinced me to join Facebook, he explained how he managed to keep in touch with his best friends Peter and Bruce:

> It's difficult for me because I'm just not the kind of person that calls somebody. I feel bad about that, you know what I mean? Peter is definitely the one in our group of friends that calls everybody and checks up on people. And I'll do that, too, sometimes, but keeping in touch is … it's difficult for me. It's really not that hard, though, to stay in touch 'cause there's Facebook and that's where we mostly talk to each other. We'll call each other on the phone, but not that often, you know, just like every once in a while. And it's never awkward, it's always really comfortable. There's been periods of time where I haven't spoken to Bruce for maybe three months and I can call him on the phone and we'll have the chillest, illest conversation 'cause like that's just how it is. We just understand each other on that level. The time apart doesn't really matter that much.

In high school, Popcorn, Peter and Bruce were inseparable. They are kind and popular young men and despite Peter and Bruce's lack of attention to schoolwork, all were liked by their teachers. The young men are aspiring artists interested in writing, photography and videography, and they produce films with and for each other. After they graduated the three were nervous about being apart from each other on such a consistent basis. For a year, Peter and Bruce attended community college together in Brooklyn; Popcorn was the one to leave New York City and this made him simultaneously sad and excited. Popcorn's self-awareness of his own shyness highlights an important part of social networking: It provides a means to keep in touch, indeed to make and maintain friendships, when direct social connections feel more difficult. A year later, in June 2011 after returning from a semester in Paris, Popcorn had a slightly different perspective on his Facebook usage:

I use Facebook because it allows me to get a glimpse into the lives and almost the minds of people I know and love, friends, family, etc. from a certain distance. On one level it makes me feel secure and happy knowing that they are doing fine depending on what their status reads or what their new photos show and the emotions expressed in those images. I'm free not to use it, but in our world it's kinda hard not to because it provides a free and easy way to connect with people (at certain distance once again) which is what I think we all want.

Being just under an hour from New York City and the majority of his social circle made Facebook a convenience; being several thousand miles away, in a foreign country, altered his use of and perspective on Facebook. He now witnessed friends and family from a significant geographic distance; Paris was the furthest he had been from home, and his time there was the longest time he had been without the presence of any long-term friends or family. Popcorn now felt a new challenge: How to make friends in a country whose language he did not speak while maintaining friendships from home. When he speaks of distance, he does so from a great distance, contributing to his shift in perspective.

The participants are so accustomed to Facebook that they do not see it as anything special or out of the ordinary. They minimize any indication that it might be "important," "different" or worthy of the concern raised by the popular press.[17] Indeed, some comments sound downright dismissive of Facebook:

Bruce: FB doesn't mean anything significant except what it is. A social network.

Peter: A distraction, an annoyance, useless.

Serenity: FB is just a fun social network.

Despite their dismissive tones, Bruce, Peter and Serenity are avid users of Facebook. Even Peter's comment that it is a "distraction, an annoyance, useless" seems to be contradicted by his frequent updates. Admittedly, Peter's most frequent posts occur during semester breaks, implying that maybe he is focused on his studies during the school year, but there is no way of knowing how often he checks Facebook. That he labels it a "distraction" might mean he checks it frequently (without posting) and calling it a distraction is a self-admonishment.

Many of the participants echo the literature that assuages parental fears about online predators or Internet stalkers.[18] The participants tend to use Facebook to keep up with already established friendships, not to make new friends:

Brick: To me Facebook is just another way of socializing. It lets you monitor what people are up to or what is going on in people's life a bit. It's a good way of keeping in contact with people. It is a way of keeping in contact not with just your friends but also with the ones that aren't in your immediate life.

Jacline: Facebook to me just means a place to catch up with old friends, and see what your friends and family are up to. I don't see it as a way to meet new friends. I meet new friends in the real world and then add them on Facebook.

Planet J observes how, because of its popularity, Facebook has become something of a requirement in today's society:

Facebook to me is just another social site that became popular to pop culture, similar to MySpace and Sconex. The only factor that makes Facebook a more useful network to me is its popularity. I am able to connect with more people because more people are familiar with it, compared to other social outlets. I am convinced that Facebook will eventually become obsolete to another social network with similar qualities.

Planet J's prediction might happen sooner rather than later. The demise of MySpace and Sconex provide a warning that Facebook should not rely on its popularity, and the development of Google+ may prove a threat to Facebook (Auletta 2011; Miller 2011). No matter what, digital communication is firmly a part of our interpersonal communication, which gives Popcorn pause:

To me Facebook means a lot of different things. It's this indefinite space where people from definite locations in the world can keep in touch and talk to each other. It's the first empire of the Internet in terms of user account sites and it's the single highest holder of personal information for a vast number of people. It's like a country or government that knows everything about its citizens. From their likes to dislikes, where they've been, where they are going, addresses, phone numbers, family structure, down to their emotional states, which is fucking scary. And I feel the name "Facebook" itself carries its own unique anxieties, problems, and questions that are fairly new to the human experience.

Popcorn sums up a major popular and scholarly concern: Facebook, and digital communication more broadly, represent a new way of communicating, and the tentacles that enable business and government entry to our (formerly) private lives are so vast as to be inconceivable.

John is the only participant who expresses concern about people's potential lack of awareness of the power of Facebook. He explains, "Facebook is a very powerful tool to me. Not many realize that, when used in the right way, it allows for the sharing of ideas and news with many and for the growth of friendship. But it can also be a dangerous thing, one must be careful." Facebook's "danger" rests in the ability to capture seemingly all facets of a person's identity and personal information. Yet, despite his caution, John posts a great deal of personal information on his Facebook page and admitted he has not configured his privacy settings.

Nino believes Facebook can be an outlet to promote her work. She made two attempts at college–a community college in New York City, then a year at a state school in Southern California–before realizing that traditional classroom learning was not for her. She now takes photography classes and works part-time to pay for photography and art supplies. Nino is a graphic artist who designed the logo for her and her friends' skate crew, Turkey Grease, and she has started a graphic design business based on this logo. Several friends and family members have Turkey Grease iron-on patches, t-shirts and even tattoos. Nino has gained a degree of recognition in her community in large part because of Facebook. When she makes a new design she posts the image on Facebook where all her friends and family can see and often repost her work:

> Sometimes when I make a cool little photoshopped turkey, I put it as my profile picture. It's just 'cause I like it so much, I want it to be my photo. And, then sometimes there's videos I've made and I'll be like, "You guys should check this out." It's really cool and I like to hear what people's thoughts are. It's not 'cause I'm marketing, I want to share something I've made, something I did with my own hands.

When her friends and family repost her work, there is potential for innumerable people to see her designs and videos. Nino dreams of a Turkey Grease artists' co-operative and wants to expand the business beyond her local community, but she knows it is she, not Facebook, who must do the expansion work:

> I haven't really done much to get people to know me, to get strangers to notice my artwork. I haven't marketed it. So I was really thinking about making a blog. It's just, I'm too lazy to set up a page and do the background. But I'm really thinking about doing that. I don't know how, but I been looking at instructions on how to build a web page and it's good for marketing my photos and artwork and maybe I could start selling stuff online. I really want to do it, I just been too lazy to actually sit down and put all the work together. But I'm really gonna do it! I don't know when.

Nino's acknowledgment that she is just lazy enough to not proactively market herself shows that, as McChesney (2005) predicted, having a digital presence does not promote democracy. Nino will not become successful *just because* she has a Facebook page and she has yet to start her blog or market her work.[19]

In line with why they use Facebook and what Facebook means to them, the participants have a relaxed attitude about how Facebook is understood in society. No one has, or is willing to share, experiences of struggles in cyberland, though many of them have shared serious personal crises with me in interviews over the years. While Facebook may be a site to play out interpersonal drama or comment on life's difficulties, no participant admits to being a cyberbully or a cybervictim. They do not see the site as anything "special," and indeed, most comment on how "mainstream" and "ordinary" it is:

Brick: I feel like Facebook in society today has become a mainstream thing. It is something that everyone almost needs or people start to think it's weird if you don't have a Facebook. It's almost like an addiction for a lot of people in society, they need to constantly check it no matter what time of day it is and sometimes every five minutes people check it, even though nothing new has happened. Another aspect is in society it really is a big socializing site. Such that, if you meet someone outside of Facebook people almost always go on Facebook to find them to add them to their friends list and get to know them that way instead of calling or talking to them in real life.

Jacline: To me Facebook is very important to this generation, many good things come from it as well as many bad things, but it's a very popular social network that is therefore important in this cyber era.

Serenity: FB is used as an outlet to get certain things off your chest, write poetry, even discuss personal business. It's like a journal or diary for some people.

It is increasingly rare, though certainly not impossible, to meet people *without* a Facebook presence and as Brick points out, it does seem "weird." Jacline's diplomatic approach–there is both good and bad–makes room for Serenity's belief that Facebook is a place to vent and share. People may complain about a loss of privacy, but with such a high number of users on a global scale, many of whom use the site "to get certain things off your chest," users are responsible for their own behavior.

Both Popcorn and John discuss the implications of digital technology on human advancement:

Popcorn: I think Facebook is the first step in which humans, having created the Internet, entirely merge with it, already evident in our dependency on it already within the past 10 years. More and more it becomes readily accessible to us and I feel that the medium or machine which we interact with–the Internet and thus each other (through the computer)–will be eliminated, and it will become a more direct experience in quickly accessing information about each other and the world.

John: Facebook has become engraved with modern society and media, it has become a tool of social change and sharing of news. The events in the Middle East is a great example, where protesters used social media like Facebook and Twitter to share with the world what has been occurring. It is the duty of owners of Facebook to remain neutral in such events, of course. It's quite a wonder this Facebook, I must say.

Both Popcorn and John talk about profound changes within the digital environment, where we are fused with technology that will ultimately change the world. Yet, on a day-to-day basis, what is most striking is how ordinary their life experiences are. Similarly, as participants graduate from high school and move into college or work they experience extraordinary changes that are lived in an ordinary way. The following four chapters present the participants and share their stories about how they remember high school, what they believe the purpose of high school is and how they make sense of their lives as they enter and move through the next phase of their lives. Unless otherwise noted, the majority of participant stories are drawn from interviews conducted through Facebook. While Facebook plays a vital part in their development, the primary purpose of the data is to illustrate the participants' self-conception and reflection on their growth. Facebook is used as a tool to gather that data.

THREE

"We Were All Like a Close Family": Remembering High School

Jacline, a young Latina about to start her fourth year of college, remembers high school as a place where her classmates, teachers and staff "were all like a close family." She appreciated the "teachers and students supporting each other," and this became a poignant memory when she felt adrift during her first term in college, away from a familiar, stable support system. Jacline was a member of the first graduating class of her high school and was excited by her acceptance to a small college about eight hours north of New York City. However, after her first year away and a decline in health that she attributed to being away from her family, Jacline transferred to a college in New York City. She wants to become an architect and feels that she will have the most success at this while also being with her family. Since switching schools and moving back to New York City, Jacline has excelled academically and has been accepted to an architectural program at a competitive city college.

Jacline's comment one repeated by the majority of the participants–illustrates a personal view of high school and reflects the school's emphasis on interpersonal connections. The majority of the participants state that they were not prepared for the transition to college, and for many, that awareness did not surface until after they had already experienced serious struggle, including flunking out, getting sick, or finding themselves debilitatingly lonely. Participants who had just finished their first year of college describe their struggles with the quantity of work and classroom expectations. Facebook is often the site where they express their frustration. The quantity and quality of comments posted by their electronic friends demonstrate that Facebook is a place of support and cohesion. During October and March (midterms) and December and May (finals) there is an increase in postings focused on school struggles.

The American ideal of leaving home for college is not one that suits young people whose high schools embrace personal connections but, for a variety of reasons, do not (or cannot) prepare them for the realities of the university classroom. Given the continued decline of the economy, the university classroom is in the midst of change, and the participants attending college feel the impact of these as yet undefined changes. The majority of the participants are the first in their families to attend college and have not experienced the invisible privilege of multigenerational college attendance. The relationship model of intimate, interpersonal connections with which they grew familiar in high school is not sustained in college. Despite the challenges they faced as underserved youth, when they were accepted and enrolled at mainstream universities, often in unfamiliar cities with little or no familial support, many participants showed they were unable to successfully make the transition. The knowledge learned on the streets of New York City did not help them in a more mainstream education environment. Participants use Facebook to share frustrations, fascinations and fears, including a developing awareness of their own personal responsibility as expressed through efforts to get to class or work on time, the balance of work and school, and their appreciation and respect for their long-term friends as they encounter and engage with new people at school and work. Facebook takes on the role of a digital support system–with near instant feedback–as they maneuver through unfamiliar terrain. This chapter draws from participants' memories to construct a portrait of what was missing in their high school and where they struggle in university and full-time labor.

Remembering High School: Joy and Dismay

All participants attended Lincoln Square High School (LSHS) on the West Side of Manhattan, described in Chapter Two. Small schools in New York City are designed with 100 or fewer students per grade, making it relatively easy to get to know, or at least be familiar with, all the students in one's grade. The intimacy fostered in a small school, expressed both in the students' peer relationships and in their relationships with teachers and staff who were stable, consistent adults in their lives is valuable to the majority of the participants. An important element of small schools is advisory, a class that operates outside the curriculum, intended to develop an intimate relationship between teachers and a small number of students, ideally over the course of the students' tenure at the school. The guiding principle of advisory is that one particular teacher will be a consistent advocate for a student's development. However, in urban schools with high teacher turnover, this relationship does not always develop as intended. Indeed, enthusiastic intention versus actual reality is an overarching theme of small school growth and development. Many participants are Facebook friends with their former high school teachers, developing a long-term digital relationship in place of a face-to-face relationship. As the participants venture forth into the world beyond the protective confines of high school, their high school memories solidify into important support systems and lessons learned.

The class of 2008 was the first graduating class; when LSHS opened in 2004, the initial 100 students, their teachers and staff were the only people in the school, testing a new formula in small-school reform. This intimacy undoubtedly fosters the close connection felt by the classmates. All the participants who graduated in 2008 comment on the close family ties and peer support system fostered in their school:

Bruce: There are too many great memories, seriously. But to choose one, I will go with when I made my movie *I Need a Mustache* and had the school in an uproar of laughter and buzzing for hours.

Nino: I would have to say my fondest memories of high school were with my friends.

Peter: Being able to know I could see Bruce and Popcorn daily. All the great teachers and staff.

Jasmine: My best memory of high school would have to be my freshman year when I met some of my closest friends today.

Johnny: My fondest memory of high school would have to be knowing everyone in my year and watching us all grow from the people we came in as into the people we left as. In my honest opinion nobody left the same way they came to LSHS.

Last: Hanging out with my best friends and watching the people I knew then, be the people they were.

Natalie: My happiest memory of high school is when we would sit like a family to address a new task or a situation. It felt like a family. It's important to feel like that in a school due to the fact that we can push each other to succeed and not be shut out by cliques or intimidation.

Planet J: My best memory of high school is the combined work of my best friend and I. Every film we created was viewed on a large projector during our media presentations in our film production classes. I remember our school enjoying every project we would produce. We were well known for our talents, and everyone enjoyed our work.

Johnny, a lithe Asian man who never did very well in school, currently works two part-time jobs in New York City after dropping out of two different community college programs. Johnny's grandmother often baked Indonesian treats that he would bring to school to share with me. He is an attentive individual who suffers from a depression significant enough to keep him from concentrating on schoolwork. Another participant, Last, barely graduated from high school; on the very afternoon of graduation he was surprised to learn that he would receive credit if he prepared a speech to give at the graduation ceremony. Receiving credit for work not actually completed is not unique to LSHS; it is a way that struggling start-up, alternative and charter schools manipulate their numbers to appear more productive and successful than they really are (Otterman 2011a). Last chose to take time off before beginning community college–as will be shown, not as much time off as he had planned. Natalie, a young Latina, did fairly well in high school but did not push herself and when she began community college, was surprised by the workload and the deadlines. She suffered significant stress, as will be discussed in Chapter Five, and her talk often reveals a desire to return to the perceived safety of high school. Jasmine, a petite Asian woman who always did well in school, now attends a private university five hours north of New York City. She made the transition to college very easily, as will be discussed in Chapter Five. She spent a semester in Florence studying culinary arts and hospitality and regularly posted pictures of sites she visited, food she prepared and friends she made. Planet J, a soft-spoken African American man, is an aspiring videographer in partnership with his best friend. While in high school, classmates always looked forward to his films; an unassuming young man, Planet J was generally pleased with the response to his films, and he felt a security in high school that he no longer feels. He has spoken to me about feeling sad and lonely since high school and he desperately wants that security back. While it is certainly important that the memories of high school include feeling good and secure, these feelings did not necessarily assist the participants in their transitions to college or work.

Most participants remember the creation of strong friendships and how these friendships were the support they needed to contend with hard times. Genevieve, a 2009 graduate, explains the importance of her friends: "If I didn't have the friends I had in high school I probably would have offed myself (to be frank). I didn't start coming into myself until I made the friends I have 'til this day. They made high school wonderful, crazy and unforgettable. I love them." Genevieve, a young African American woman, initially attended a private school north of New York City but failed her first semester, which will be discussed in greater detail over the next few chapters.

The most recent graduates were the class that made LSHS complete. The graduates of 2010 were the last of the first: When they began ninth grade in 2007, the school had a complete four-year student body. They, too, comment on the importance of friendship and interpersonal connections:

Brick: A fondest memory from high school is giving the Valedictorian speech. I was able to overcome a fear of standing in front of an audience and giving a speech.

John: My greatest memory of high school was the kindness and dedication of the teachers. Also, the opportunity I was given to attend summer boarding school. Also the valuable life lessons I learned through those 4 years and my growth.

Hass: The best memory would be our senior trip. During my senior year I got to know ALL my friends and teachers very well because we spent three days together and played manhunt in which the teachers acted like teens again and it was a great experience.

Helena: One great memory was just having people there for me with all their support.

Hass, a young Latino, was divided in his behavior in high school: He had gang connections and sometimes worked to be hard; at other times he was more interested in fun activities such as connecting with classmates and teachers. During his sophomore year he was never on time to school and almost had to repeat the grade because he missed so much classtime. Helena, a young Latina, took a long time to be comfortable in high school. It was not until 11th grade, when she discovered an interest in photography that she came into her own. In 10th grade she had a serious boyfriend who was a senior; when he broke up with her because he was getting ready to graduate, she was devastated and spent most days crying. However, when she pulled herself out of this malaise, she discovered her friends again and was soon more social and happy. She has an overprotective father who made her phone him every morning when she arrived at school. Because cell phones were not allowed, she had to get permission to use staff members' phones, and this was a source of great embarrassment for her.

One participant, Pink, did not graduate from LSHS. She experienced such a difficult first year, with a significant number of disciplinary and academic problems, that she was forced to repeat the ninth grade. During her second year in the ninth grade she was so resentful of being held back that she rarely attended school and ultimately dropped out. She had significant interpersonal problems with the principal and the majority of the administrative staff and was a veritable stranger to her teachers, often showing up only to antagonize classmates or check in with friends. Nevertheless, she does have fond memories of her first time as a ninth grader, explaining, "My best memory of high school would have to be my freshman year, I connected with teachers we had a lot of nice trips; it was a exciting year." After acknowledging her tribulations and taking responsibility for her role as troublemaker, she realizes, "Going through high school was a good experience after all."

Memories of high school are not always positive, especially in a school as tumultuous as LSHS. In its first four years, the principal was an enthusiastic woman of uneven leadership skills. She was known to change the curriculum regularly and antagonized faculty, staff and students alike. The students, having no other high school experience against which to judge this situation, assumed it was normal. Some resented the perceived lack of opportunities. As the literature on alternative and charter schools indicates, the enthusiasm for starting a new school is difficult to maintain while running the school day to day (Wells 2002). What seems good and productive with 100 students is untenable with 400. For example, Pink remembers "a lot of nice trips" her first year in high school; there were field trips around the city almost every week when there were only 100 students. By the time there were 400 students, including students who needed to prepare for state-required exams, SATs and college applications, weekly all-grade field trips were no longer possible.

For the most part, the participants' most difficult memories of high school revolve around the general stress of testing and graduation preparation, a familiar experience for many high school students:

Brick: I would have to say my roughest memory is a lot of 12th grade due to stress and being really hard for me to get through. The reason I felt so stressed was because of college applications on top of the work from classes. I was really lost. I mean I know it was only 12th grade but I felt like I had no clue what I was going to do with my life and it really took a toll on me. I was and still am scared of the future. Not to mention also senioritis was a pain. It's normal but it just made it worse because I had to force myself to do my work and get it done.

Genevieve: Senior year. For me personally, I felt I made some bad choices in terms of what I was gonna do after I graduated and what kind of person I was gonna be. In senior year, I caught a glimpse of it, and it wasn't pretty. I let myself go, my grades went down, and I didn't take anything as serious as I should have. I was sort of in a paralyzed position mostly because I had this fear of leaving this state of comfort. High school and my friends were my life, my cocoon. Once senior year was beginning to end, it was as if I was losing my shelter and my comfort and I started to panic and I sort of froze in place. I was trying to stand still as if life would also, but it didn't. It just kept on going and with me pretending like it didn't, it had repercussions I still to this day regret.

Though Brick and Genevieve have very different families and backgrounds, they share some important similarities. Brick, one of the few white students at LSHS, has two parents who are very supportive of his desires but have little experience themselves with college or college preparation. Genevieve, an African American raised by a single mother in a multigenerational household with her grandmother and a brother with a significant mental disability, has no family member with any successful college experience. With a conspicuous absence of college matriculation by their parents or older generations, Brick and Genevieve are the first in their families to test the experience. Brick's perspective that it was "only 12th grade" is countered by his feelings of being lost and scared. Genevieve retreated to her "cocoon" of friends because most of them shared similar feelings.

Many of the participants saw the end of high school as a betrayal of their heretofore firm belief in how the world worked. Bruce recalls a particularly difficult time when he realized one of his close friends would not be graduating:

Bad memory has to be when, on graduation day, I found out my friend wasn't graduating. My understanding for why he didn't graduate is because he didn't fulfill the requirements. It bothered me because in other peoples' eyes I became superior because of my achievements and it's not the case because academic achievements don't show the value of a man.

For Bruce, this was the first time he experienced being "better" than someone close to him, for what he believed was an arbitrary reason. Throughout high school all students had been supported, but graduation revealed that divisions existed despite that emotional support.

Many participants have bad memories of getting into trouble for infractions real or perceived and struggling with the consequences. The consequences felt bad but also taught the participants how to deal with conflict, especially with adult authority figures. Serenity was a well-behaved student who had no disciplinary problems. She does remember one troubling interaction with the principal that made her angry:

My worst memory of high school was when my principal tried to suspend me for a hairstyle. It was in a 'deubie,' which is basically a hair wrap with bobby pins. She said it was inappropriate and ghetto. I fought her on the situation and went as far as to almost get the superintendent involved. A hairstyle? Like come on let's be serious, it wasn't like I had a hat on, just bobby pins with my hair wrapped.

Serenity's story is a specific example of the confusing policies of the principal and a more general example of how young people learn the boundaries set by adult authority figures: How does one practice self-expression while also adhering to the expectations of the larger environment? In any school, the principal is the authority figure who sets the tone for the school. In part because the first principal of LSHS started at the same time as the first graduating class, students felt a close, if conflicted, relationship with her. Some participants feel more anger towards the principal, either as an individual or as a representation of the power structure of high school. Peter, a member of the first graduating class and witness to many of the principal's infractions, laments that his worst memory was watching the principal "destroy the school, when I realized how amazing LSHS was in the beginning and seeing what it became by the time I graduated." Peter chooses not to be more specific than this, but his frustration highlights a valuable lesson in conflict management and where to search for the roots of conflict. The principal was undoubtedly not responsible for all the school's struggles, but as the leader of the start-up school, she is the clearest figure for the students to blame when they feel slighted.

Not surprisingly, many participants speak vaguely about negative interpersonal squabbles during high school that are representative of peer-to-peer conflict management:

> *Helena:* My toughest time in high school was when people judged me before they met me. There were certain things that were happening at the time and certain people thought false statements that bothered me because some of them never even knew me. It hurt a lot because I would never judge someone, especially if I didn't know them. There's a difference between thinking something that someone might be and not knowing if they are that type of person but to put a final judgment on them and saying they're this or that is wrong and it hurts because you don't know them like that. There are always two sides of the story and whether you know someone or not you should always be open to knowing what everyone says isn't true. If you don't know for sure keep your mouth closed.

> *John:* I had a hard time with a certain group of students who would be very disrespectful and seem to not have a clear goal in life, who had no respect for others. Also my bad performance on some important tests.

> *Nino:* One day during lunch in 10th grade I was publicly notified about the infidelities that took place between my boyfriend and a girl in my class. It was a very embarrassing moment that became even worse when our guidance counselor wanted to intervene.

In the age of digital media, these squabbles can be played out instantly—and archived permanently—online. Facebook was only newly available when these young people were in high school, so truly seamless digital communication was yet to exist. The participants were relieved, upon reflection, that the negative experiences they remember occurred before they had Facebook pages, therefore many negative interactions remained within the walls of the school and with the impermanence of traditional interpersonal communication. Furthermore, because Helena, John and Nino also articulated positive interpersonal memories, what is revealed is not surprising: High school is a complex place where both conflict and joy are experienced. Increased digital media have heightened and accelerated the experience of conflict and harmony, not eliminated them.

One of the challenges of attending a small start-up school is that there are generally fewer opportunities to participate in "traditional" high school activities. Building a school culture beyond interpersonal connections is difficult, and making space, or allotting money for fringe activities, is challenging. The class of 2008 had worked for a year on their yearbook before its production was halted with no explanation. Unsuccessful attempts were made to salvage the work into a digital yearbook. Instead, the students were presented with what Bruce named, in disgust, a "yearfolder," a collection of photos and poems that were photocopied at the last minute. It was a source of frustration and embarrassment for the students who knew enough about high school to know that a yearbook is a traditional, mainstream means to preserve memory—one they would not have. Calmly, Jacline recollects that this was the hardest memory for her of high school, "We worked so hard as a group to make our senior yearbook and there was no yearbook. All the hard work and looking forward to it and there was nothing."

Some of the participants suffered significant mental health struggles that were not appropriately addressed by the high school administrators. Given some of the difficulties these young people faced, bouts of depression were not surprising. The participants remember some of the consequences negatively:

Johnny: In freshman year, I had to go to counseling and deal with child services for falling asleep in class. That was mad embarrassing.

Last: I hit a very deep depression at the start of my senior year. I didn't like seeing people watch me change into the depressive creature I eventually became.

Both Johnny and Last almost did not graduate from high school. The experiences of these two young men demonstrate the achievement gap that develops because of the absence of effective social services before school begins (Wilder, Allgood & Rothstein 2008) and the resultant embarrassment when private struggles are made public. In a small school, there is little room to hide or be invisible, yet many struggles go without acknowledgment and are not dealt with by the appropriate staff.

Some participants admit to unhealthy and risky choices they made in high school, and they look back on them with a critical distance that takes account of lessons learned from the consequences of their actions:

Natalie: I got caught with alcohol in school. I felt like it was something I didn't want to be perceived as. But it also helped me grow as a person. Even though I brought the alcohol to school on accident it humbled me as a person because it taught me the consequences to my actions.

Pink: My second year as a 9th grader I felt like I was not gonna make it. I had to repeat that grade and I kept getting suspended. I was more out of school than in school. I would go to school for like two weeks and get suspended for like a month, and a lot of things changed in those months I was suspended, because every time I would go back I just kept having more trouble keeping up with my school work because it would get accumulated.

Lucy: My worst memory would have to be when you found that book I thought my life was going to be over! I thought you were going to tell the principal, I thought my mom was going to find out, worst feeling ever!

Lucy, who graduated in 2009, refers to a journal she kept chronicling her drug use. She forgot this journal in my office one day and because I returned it to her without "snitching" she grew to trust me. When Lucy stopped doing drugs for a brief period, she used the journal as a tangible memory of a place to which she did not want to return. Pink took just about two years to get her life straightened out and return to school, and she remembers that time as an important life lesson. Natalie never again took such a risk in school; she paid closer attention to the choices she made, thinking of their consequences. All these young women use these experiences as benchmarks for behavioral choices they make today.

Pivotal Personal Moments: High School

There is no doubt that high school is a time when young people experience pivotal moments of change whose memories remain with them for the rest of their lives. Some of those moments are positive, and some profoundly negative.

Pink, who was held back to repeat the ninth grade, ultimately chose to drop out of high school. When I first met Pink in fall 2006, her attendance was sporadic at best. She was rumored to have deep gang connections and was regularly in altercations with the principal and staff. Pink was clearly an intelligent young woman but was also extremely manipulative and paid no heed to any adult's attempt at discipline. When she attended school she spent most of the day in the bathroom avoiding classes, or she might interrupt classes if she wanted to check in with friends. She appeared in school one day with what looked like a brand burned into her hand, and the rumor spread that this was her gang member boyfriend's initial. Sighing at the memory, Pink explains:

When I was in LSHS I didn't have a boyfriend's name branded on my hand. I actually never had a boyfriend. The real story behind that is that I was in my house trying to cook–back then I had no idea how–I ended up letting water fall in hot oil and I got it on my hand and it was a horrible burning feeling. I scratched it so much that my skin got irritated the next day when I went to school the principal approached me and she asked me what happened to my hand, but before I could even reply, she assumed that I branded someone's name. I never actually branded anything on my hand, but I let her think that by not clearing things up for her.

It remains unclear why anyone would assume the burn was an intentional brand. Undoubtedly the rumor, whether true or false, made Pink more intimidating to her classmates. Though she claims there was no boyfriend—in the midst of dropping out of high school, Pink also came out as a lesbian—she did have deep gang connections, so it was easy to believe the story without any direct denial or corroboration. Pink maintains that while she was "involved" in the gang, she was never an official member:

> When I was attending LSHS I was involved in a gang but I was never a member of it. I used to meet up with those people during school and get myself in trouble and then get myself in trouble again with my parents for coming home late. All I did was fight and argue for people who at the end of the day weren't doing anything for me but cause me more problems than what I already had. As time went by I started separating myself from them, I started thinking of my future and I saw how I was wasting my time hanging out with them instead of looking for a school. When I got back into school, I discovered how passionate I am about reading, I didn't have any problems at home because I wouldn't be home as late as before. My goal was to get my high school diploma. I felt like this was the last chance I had and if I didn't think wisely and did something for myself now I wasn't gonna be able to do it later on.

Upon reflection, Pink, who regularly posts to Facebook about the importance of owning one's own sexual identity and comments at length about sexual politics and the rights of gay and lesbian people, believes her struggles at LSHS and in the gang were worth it to help her learn more:

> Today I am a completely different person compared to who I was back then. Work and school are my priorities. The people I am surrounded by are the opposite of the people I used to associate myself with back then. I truly believe that all the experiences that we go through along the road is what helps us appreciate the journey.

Pivotal experiences do not need to be negative in order to make a lasting impression. John, a deeply emotional young man whose intelligence can be muddled by his exaggerated expressions, had an opportunity to attend summer school at an elite private school in New England the summer after his sophomore year in high school. John followed in the footsteps of five of his classmates who had attended the program in the previous two years, and he was terribly excited to attend. He knew enough from his elder classmates that the transition would be difficult and that the academic expectations would be extremely challenging, which might set off his emotional outbursts. However, he was so excited for the opportunity that he worked diligently to maintain his composure and made sure to have support systems he could reach out to in times of struggle. In August 2008 he sent me pictures of the friends he had made and thanked me for helping him complete his application and plan his travels:

> Thank you so very much for giving me this kind of opportunity. I had the time of my life and made friendships which I'm sure will last a lifetime. I learned so much and I feel smarter and I feel more responsible as a young man. I believe that this experience has changed me quite a bit. Thank you, from the bottom of my heart for everything and for helping me reach this goal.

Reflecting on his high school experience, he remembered the summer program fondly. Two years after his initial thanks to me for my role in helping him get there, he still remembered the summer with great joy, so much so that he encouraged a classmate to attend and supported her through her initial homesickness:

> My experience was phenomenal. I experienced something that you just experience once and that it changes you, it matures you and it sets you straight, it shows you the world. By that I mean people from around the world come together for a month to learn and become close. You learn to accept other cultures and you learn about yourself and the kind of person you really are. That's why I encouraged a friend of mine to sign up and try her best. She was doubtful and reluctant but I convinced her. First week she was homesick and whatnot but now she does not want to go home, she loves it! I told her I wanted her to experience and feel what I felt. She has grown and that's what the program does. I wish so many people could experience these things. You learn how important education is and how powerful it can be in a person's life. I also learned that in this world, sometimes connections are the best way to go in life. You also learn about your emotions and the power of friendship, about who is real and who is not.

In many ways, John's story echoes the American ideal of leaving home for college and using the opportunity to engage with previously unfamiliar social and intellectual activities (Arnett 2004). Given his financial and immigration struggles, the summer school experience may be John's only opportunity with this breadth of learning.

Brick and John, both 2010 graduates, were the valedictorian and salutatorian, respectively, of their graduating class. They each expressed to me the joy and trepidation they felt at giving their speeches to the auditorium of classmates, family, teachers and friends:

> *Brick:* I ended up talking about the future. But more in the sense that it is our turn to define who we are and how we want our life to be. Also, that even if we don't know what path we want to take that it is okay and that we will find what we want to do with our lives in the next four years of school. I also mentioned that we are the next generation to take responsibility for running the United States. Our responsibilities are greater than just thinking about ourselves, and we should think about how we want to affect our family, friends and community.

John: Writing my salutatorian speech proved more difficult that I initially thought, I spent restless nights trying to find inspiration and a message. I knew it had something with being optimistic and strong and moving forward because it is a core value, along with being kind, but I also needed to see what it was I found bothersome, that made me sad. It started to take shape: The kindness, the hate, society and its mentality, people giving up on themselves and that's when I remembered the word *invictus*, which is Latin for undefeated and I decided that would be my hook and I would write my soul out from there.

It is clear that by graduation, Brick's "senioritis" stress and fear had transformed into more focused, clear plans. John still appeared to be determined to tackle all his passions in one speech. Both young men used the opportunity to solidify their thoughts and feelings. They reflected on the writing process and how they came to prepare their work:

Brick: I had help from my family. They helped me write it and helped me with the ideas. I had the idea I wanted to talk about the future. I had a couple of quotes in mind that I wanted to use to help me with the direction of my speech. Then my brother told me maybe I should bring it in the direction of responsibility and ambitions. And my parents then helped me write the paper.

John: I looked up quotes related to the topics hate, love, religion and kindness. I shared it with some friends who read it and suggested changes and better ways to say things, so I took their suggestions and then presented it to the principal who loved it and another staff member who gave me tips on how to write it, bold letters and bigger letters for the emphasis I wanted.

In addition, both young men posted their speeches on Facebook where any electronic friend could read them.

Post-High School Plans

The 2010 graduates spoke most speculatively about their post-high school plans. The other participants looked back on their post-graduation transitions with the benefit of time and experiences, and they have already begun to revise and polish their narratives. The participants who graduated in 2010 answered questions about their plans within a week of graduating, so there is a rawness to their expectations. Their plans are varied:

Brick: I just graduated high school so my plans are to go off to college and find what I will enjoy to do for a career.

Helena: I plan on starting college in the fall. I chose my school because the major they had seemed very similar to what I want to be doing in the future. I love the location of the school and feel that I will fit just right in. I also love how I can double major in two things that interest me the most. I will be living at home since the school is very close to where I live.

Hass: After graduation I will work for the summer and then leave for the Marines. I want to go to the Marines because I don't want to go to college and in the Marines I get paid good money. I want to get away from New York and also to challenge myself into reaching my goal of doing something I always wanted to do.

John: As of now I'm debating whether taking a year off school, I don't feel 100%. What I'm doing for college is part my decision and the other part not my decision, part of why I'm not attending first semester is for financial reasons and others private.

A year later, both Brick and Helena had made their plans concrete. After some initial struggles, Brick had a successful first year in a private college just north of the city. He is thoroughly enjoying his time there and regularly posts pictures on Facebook of life in "the country," what he calls his new environment outside of New York City. Helena's interest in fashion photography was realized at the private school she attends. She regularly posts artistic portraits of friends and carefully constructed self-portraits on her Facebook page. Hass has yet to sign up for the Marines, despite his initial desire to leave New York, make money and realize his unspecified goals. He has stayed in New York City, has a serious girlfriend, and works at a series of low-skilled part-time jobs. Judging from his Facebook posts, he spends much of baseball season watching Yankee games and getting high with his friends. After all of John's excitement about school, bolstered especially by his summer private boarding school and salutatorian experiences, he was vague about attending college. He and his family struggle financially; more pertinently, he is afraid that his family's illegal status will be revealed if he applies for college. He explains, "My documents are not in order. They are being taken care of but as of now I'm undocumented. But we're taking care of everything as best as possible." John very much wants what he imagines to be the "regular college experience," as he puts it:

Just being able to go as a regular student and just do and experience everything a freshman should experience. When your friends are going far away and doing their thing, you sort of experience jealousy and wanting to succeed yourself. But I gotta be strong and know that it takes time to succeed and get to where I want to be.

In the meantime, John works at his uncle's bodega, babysits his nieces and advances his reading and math on his own.

For many of the participants, graduating from high school and moving to new education or work experiences is an invitation to reflect on the nature and reality of their high school. The most recent graduates explain their high school in practical, matter-of-fact terminology:

> *Brick:* The school tries to incorporate media into the curriculum. They have very dedicated teachers that are there for the students no matter what. They have their doors open to all the kids whether it is help with work or needing someone to talk to about life outside of school.

> *Hass:* My high school is a school in which you can learn a lot of things about the media and how it affects our lives and everyone makes you feel like you're home, especially the teachers.

> *Helena:* It is definitely not the high schools you see it on TV. It's very hectic and can get very frustrating.

> *John:* LSHS is a unique high school, it's different in that it is very small unlike the typical NYC high school. The staff and the students know each other on a first-name basis and can interact at a different level otherwise impossible in a bigger school. The small scale of it allows for more one-on-one time and the students are able to interact at a deeper level and grow from that and become better educated in being a close community.

Despite their talk about learning about the media, participants do not reveal a critical understanding of media industries. In Chapter Two I show that most participants accepted Facebook in their lives as a normal, natural conduit for communication. That so few participants are able to critique a medium with which they are intimately involved reveals an absence of critical media awareness. Furthermore, even when discussing the media theme of their high school, participants emphasize the interpersonal connections with faculty and staff. The students of LSHS learn how to make videos and are invited to analyze their process but are not taught critical media analysis. This might explain in part why they feel Facebook is such an ordinary part of their daily lives.

Those who have graduated and moved on see the school with a bit more critical distance. Genevieve explains:

> My high school was a four-year program for inner city youth. It gave us some work to keep us busy, food so we wouldn't starve. But it wasn't a real high school to me. It didn't have any challenging courses or programs. It was a school that didn't work to excel in life but to just get by enough to graduate.

That Genevieve refers to her school as a place that provided "food so we wouldn't starve" illustrates the dispossessed education that dispossessed youth receive (Freire 1970/2000): Enough to get by, but not to flourish.

Genevieve's classmate and friend Snapper, a young African American man who graduated in 2009, echoes her concerns, focusing on the disciplinary emphasis of urban schools:

> I think the best way to describe it would be a daycare center inside of a jail. That was always a joke between me and my classmates and we realized it was actually pretty true. Going to an urban school we were treated a lot differently. We had our bags scanned, went through metal detectors. It was like visiting someone in jail. But when you get down to our school you see all of these different colored rooms and the staff chasing after kids. It kinda feels like you stepped into a day care center.

Snapper attended a state university three hours north of New York City. He is interested in engineering, especially transportation. After his first year away, Snapper and his mom could no longer afford the tuition. He has since transferred to a vocational college in New York City and has a part-time job working for the New York City Transit Authority. He has a series of photo albums on his Facebook page of sights in and around New York City, which he updates regularly. He spends a lot of time on the subway for his job and as a commuter and regularly posts the amusing things, people and interactions he witnesses.

Lucy also commented on the jail-like environment of the school, calling LSHS "Mad ghetto. A prison without windows and security left and right." Space is always a struggle in New York City; it is not uncommon, especially in the era of small schools, to have multiple schools configured in one building. LSHS is one of seven schools in a building previously home to a notoriously troubled large single school that was dismantled and its students reassigned to other schools. When new small schools moved in, students were confined to single floors or sections of floors. LSHS is located in the basement of the building, with no natural light. All students from all seven schools, approximately 3,000 people, enter through the same doors framed by metal detectors and security guards with scanning wands, before being funneled to their individual schools. Some participants feel this configuration deserves explanation:

> *Natalie:* It was a very tight community, like a family. Even though we didn't have our own building we felt like we did because once we were on our floor it was a whole different setting then the rest of the building. It was warm, friendly, and comforting. If you need help with anything all you needed to do was ask a staff member. If you need to talk just stay after school and anyone of the teachers would be glad to hear you out. There's no other word to describe other than family.

> *Nino:* It's weird to explain it because my school was new and it didn't really compare to other schools in NYC. I would have to explain how each floor in the

building was a different school. My school was so small there was about 20 kids in each class and I didn't have the choice to choose my own classes.

Students disliked the scanning and having their stuff poked through every morning, but like much else, it became part of the routine. That Natalie remembers the space as a place of community and family reveals her current discomfort and struggle with increased stress and responsibility. Nino was always resentful that she had no choice of classes, an ongoing issue in small school culture. As students at highly functional, well-funded schools think about college, they may choose high school courses that will benefit their preparation. Small schools such as LSHS do not (and often cannot) offer multiple choices, leaving students systematically less prepared than their peers.

Small schools often emphasize the interpersonal connections that many of the participants have spoken about, which was a source of comfort and security for them:

Jasmine: Since LSHS has only an enrollment of 100 students per grade, students build close relationships with the principal, teachers, and other staff members while improving their academic grades.

Johnny: My high school was basically like a small community where everyone knew each other. Since we only had about 100 kids per grade everyone tried to help each other out. We did not have any stereotypical groups that one would expect to deal with in a big high school.

That interpersonal connection took some getting used to, as Serenity explains: "I thought my school was a little weird at first. The whole first-name thing shocked me, because I was always taught to say 'Ms.' and 'Mr.' to your elders. After a while my high school grew on me, the mission of the school was different and unique." However, interpersonal connections do not necessarily translate to preparation for life after high school.

What Would Make High School Better?

While Chapter One showed that scholars, critics and the popular press cannot agree on what will guarantee success of secondary schools, the participants draw from their experiences to imagine a better high school. Despite their overall fondness for their school, some of the participants have clear ideas about what would make high school better. Genevieve, Helena, Bruce and Popcorn speak at length about the problems in their high school and what should be changed.

Genevieve and Helena speak about the necessity of having multiple options, in academics, social opportunities and extracurricular activities:

Genevieve: I would have liked to have gone to a school with a lot more support systems. We know we have to pass a certain curriculum to graduate, so to give that test, but also say, "Okay, I know you're having difficulties in certain classes, so here are tutoring programs," or, "Here's extracurricular activities," just, a lot more programs to get the students engaged. I know the academics are overwhelming enough as it is, but to not have anything after school to back that up, just to make the student well-rounded. If you just give them the academics then they're gonna feel overwhelmed. So just to have a little bit of both combinations: Have a rigorous curriculum and also have that, you know, nurturing and be diverse and fun after-school programs that cater to students' interests. Also AP courses, my school didn't have AP courses. And a lot of people weren't challenged and that sort of led to them not excel in school.

Helena: High school wasn't what I thought it would be. I thought there would be more dances, trips that actually related to the school's theme since it was a media school. I thought internships would be offered to us but they weren't at all, I thought we would gain some type of more connections with media, but we didn't get that at all and that made me very angry because I felt that I was cheated out of an experience that could have bettered me in the long run. I only stayed at the school because I knew it was new and figured I would give it a chance to see what happens, but not much happened at all. And the fact that we had to go through scanning every day made me really mad because sometimes it did feel like you were a criminal in your own school, first thing in the morning and going through scanning with some security guards who were rude wasn't the best wake-up call to wanting to learn.

These young women do not have access to data about the financial organization of small schools: Small schools are permitted discretionary use of their funding, but ultimately, there is little funding. Advanced Placement courses, extracurricular activities and field trips all cost a lot of money that small schools in impoverished communities or serving dispossessed youth do not have. The security measures Helena, Snapper and Lucy discuss were touted as making young people safer, but young people who are doing no wrong are punished for infractions made by others years ago or for infractions that *might* happen, and undoubtedly they start each school day with negative feelings. When young people walk into their school and are punished preemptively every day, school becomes a threatening, not enlightening, place.

One year after their graduation, in May 2009, Bruce and Popcorn continued a debate they had been having for several years regarding who, or what, is responsible for the successes and struggles of their specific school and the larger school system. Bruce explained:

The system itself should change. That's hard to say because the Board of Education has been established for so long. So the system approved our high school, 'cause they had this plan of getting kids off the streets and into school. But, they're lessening the achievement bar of what these kids actually need to do. The building LSHS was in back in the day, that whole school was one school. And that school has like seven floors to it, so when you break something that massive down, to seven separate high schools, you're lowering the bar for these kids. So you don't expect these kids to do too much 'cause you want them in high school, you want them off the streets. So, you're getting these kids off the street, but you're just putting them through four years of nothing 'cause after, some go to college and stay in college, some go to college and drop out and then there's those who just don't go to college.

For Bruce, "you" and "they" are members of the larger Department of Education who make decisions that he feels have a negative impact on his and his classmates' experience of high school. For Bruce, "the system" is run by individuals who could–but do not–make better choices. He echoes Giroux's (2009b, 2010b) concerns about high school as a pipeline: Students are not on the streets, yet they are not challenged in classrooms either. Rather, they are funneled through a broken system. Popcorn spoke about a more abstract institution that gets caught up in a decision-making struggle:

> The thing is this, in order for the system to be changed, you have to think about it like this: Don't think about the past, or the future, just think about what's going on now. That's why we don't figure things out, because we look at the past or the future because those aren't accurate, like, things to observe. The past isn't always 100% accurate and the future, we just don't know. We only know what's going on now, so examine that, examine how the system is, not how it was or how it will be, just like how it is and just like based on how it is, like see what's unacceptable and see what works and see what doesn't work, keep those things and move those things, then take away those other things.

Popcorn's statement demands that "the system" pay attention, regularly, to the present state of multiple affairs. Yet, for the most part, students, families and increasingly their teachers are shielded from the maneuverings of the system. No participant mentioned increased testing or judging their teachers based on their own performance. All wanted more options, which were denied to them because their school had little funding. However, all did ultimately graduate and in so doing, prepared themselves for life after high school.

Chapters Four, Five and Six discuss memories of high school, the purpose of high school and the transition to college and work. In June 2010, just after high school graduation, Brick excitedly predicted, "I think college will place me on the right path. It will open my eyes to a new world. To a place I will have never even thought to have imagined before. It will be great!!!" The next chapters explore whether this proves true for Brick and his peers.

FOUR

"To Discover Yourself": Discussing the Purpose of High School

Helena, a young Latina who lives on the Lower East Side of Manhattan with her mother, recently finished her first year of college at a private school focused on the arts. She is particularly interested in photography and her Facebook page is home to several digital photo albums of self-portraits, portraits of her friends, and landscape shots of New York City. Helena believes that the purpose of high school is self-discovery. She shares stories of her own path to self-awareness and self-acceptance, often in the face of struggle:

> The purpose of high school is to learn about many things you will need to know for the future as well as challenging yourself with hard classes so you know what you need to work on. Also to learn about the world around us and taking classes that can help lead us to our future careers. To discover yourself, the type of people you hang out with, how you create yourself as an individual and going through many things that help shape you as a person.

When Helena discovered photography, she found a place of strength and motivation within herself. That process of self-discovery, she believes, got her accepted to college, but it does not make university-level learning easy. She regularly posts updates about her enthusiasm for her photography classes while lamenting the more "traditional" core courses.

The process of self-discovery, an important part of any identity project, is not supported by mainstream educational expectations where those who are in positions of unearned privilege or unearned power have a greater luxury to test out identities. The participants in this study operate without invisible privilege, yet they demonstrate that they are extraordinarily resilient individuals. They struggle at the fringes of mainstream society while working diligently to make inroads. Seven of the participants have switched schools and in so doing, have met with better academic and social success. This chapter shows that if high schools with students on the fringes of mainstream society continue to focus only superficially on college and work readiness, class divisions will continue to grow to such a degree that no amount of political rhetoric will bridge them.

The Purpose of High School

With a few months or a few years to reflect, the participants gained a critical perspective on the purpose of high school. Despite the problems in their school, it was a familiar and reliable place for them. As the 2010 graduates prepared for life beyond high school and the 2008 and 2009 graduates made adjustments to college or work environments, they looked back with critical distance to discuss the purpose of high school. None of the participants felt that high school mattered in and of itself–rather its role is preparation for life *after* high school–and opinions were mixed on how it did its job:

> *Brick:* I feel the purpose of high school is to prepare us for the world outside. To give us the knowledge we need to decide what we want to do with our lives after high school.

> *Hass:* I think that the purpose of high school is to prepare us for college or for the outside world because we become more independent.

> *John:* High school is a very important stage in a person's life, it teaches the essential skills needed in life to progress and grow. High school is for the acquiring of knowledge, the discovering of oneself and of others. It is where you learn about the world, where you grow and develop who you are and where you learn what you wish to pursue in life, to change the world for the better. From there college is to solidify who you are and grow into who you want to become.

> *Snapper:* To me, high school is all about finding yourself. Sure you learn and everything, but you make a lot of decisions while in high school. Your life starts going through a lot of changes and a lot of things start happening. For me, high school was more like learning to ride a bike without the training wheels. Once I graduated, it was like I was just pushed forward and started riding on my own.

These young men echo Helena's words about self-discovery and preparation for the "world outside." They desire challenge, want to work hard and look forward to independence, yet they are given few tools to do the necessary work to make their process of transition successful. As in their discussion in Chapter Three about what would make high school better, no participant mentioned increased testing or ways to garner a more efficient exchange of capital, yet these are prominent discussions in the current debates about education reform. All participants have fond memories of their teachers, but fond memories do not automatically translate to solid classroom performance. Both Jacline and Jasmine speak about high school as preparation for college and as a place for discovery:

> *Jacline:* To me the purpose of high school is to get a well-rounded education that prepares you for college and the real world. Ours was a small school so it focused more on the individual.

> *Jasmine:* High school helps and guides students to discover their interests in specific academic fields. High school also prepares students for college by taking required tests and writing essays. Students are encouraged to participate in various high school programs and extracurricular activities to allow them to become more involved in their school community, partake in many organization/club positions, and define their self-identity.

Many participants appreciate that they attended a city high school, which they believe instills a broader perspective of the world than schools in nonurban areas:

> *Bruce:* The main purpose of high school is prep for the challenges to come. Going to a city high school has made me more cultured.

> *Johnny:* High school is a place where you meet people you would least expect to be friends with. It is also a place that helps you find who you wanna become in the future. Not just career-wise but personally as well. I loved attending a city high school because if it weren't for that I wouldn't have the broad perspective I have now.

Johnny's comment that at high school "you meet people would least expect to be friends with" is characteristic of the experience of attending a small school in a large urban environment which draws students from all over the city. Both Johnny and Bruce commuted nearly an hour, from Queens and Brooklyn, respectively, to attend school on the West Side of Manhattan. Despite not leaving New York City, they feel their perspective is as broad as it needs to be *because* they were in New York City.

Natalie also comments that high school is a place for preparation:

> The purpose of high school is to prepare you for the world that you will be thrown into once you're out of high school. It arms you with skills that will be of great use once you become a professional or obtain a job. I enjoyed attending a city high school. Throughout my elementary and middle school education I was under close watch from my family because I always attended school in Brooklyn.

Attending high school in the city was like an open door where I could explore a whole new world by myself.

Like Johnny, Bruce and several of the participants, Natalie had a significant commute to school every day. While at times frustrating, the commute enables a certain independence and responsibility at a young age. Natalie's comment that high school prepares young people for a professional career leaves out the necessity of college. It is difficult to imagine garnering successful, professional employment without a college degree, yet for the majority of participants, to become a "professional" is to have the job security which, in the ideal situation, is what they see in their parent/guardians.

Snapper also enjoyed attending a city school, but felt that in doing so, he missed out on the traditional ideal of high school:

I enjoyed attending a city school but there were things that just made me feel like we were expected to be a certain way. I've always wanted to attend one of those high schools like in the movies but my school was special in its own way, it had a home feel to it once you got past security.

What Snapper reveals is that the *idea* of high school is often more romantic than the actuality of high school. Again, a lack of critical media literacy is revealed in Snapper's statement about attending a school "like in the movies." Unable to see that high schools in films are carefully constructed representations of a largely nonexistent ideal, Snapper longs for the image. And though he states it in an offhand way, Snapper's last comment reveals a great deal about one issue that frustrated all participants: The constant presence of security in their high school. Every morning, all students had to enter through metal detectors and submit to scanning by security officers. With students from seven schools entering one building, the morning entry was crowded and slow, a profoundly negative way to start the school day. This is an increasingly familiar feature of urban school environments.

Genevieve feels that high school is designed to teach independence:

I believe the purpose of high school is to learn just enough about life in order to survive in it alone. It is the last step before you head off into adulthood and it is very important because of that. Most of my education during high school didn't so much take place inside of the classroom but outside of it. High school was the time where I learned most about family and how growing up would affect my relationship with them. High school and the opportunities I got to experience because of it influenced my interests in media studies, music, writing and my education. I loved high school because it allowed me to discover my potential and I didn't like it because I wasn't able to exercise my potential the way I wanted to. It was bittersweet for me.

Genevieve makes the important observation that she learned about family and friendship and her own intellectual interests beyond the walls of the classroom. Her description of her experience as "bittersweet" reveals Genevieve's desire to do more, despite the disheartening obstacles in her way. For Genevieve, high school is about time, not just about the experiences within the classroom walls. The organizing principle of time is important for participants with life-altering experiences.

Lucy, for example, sees her time in high school as what gave her the courage to be public about her sexuality. She explains, "I came out in high school, freshman year. If it weren't for high school I would still be in the closet. High school to me is when teenagers find themselves, when the toughest situations occur and that's when reality kicks in."

Referring back to Snapper's comment that he wished he went to a high school "like in the movies," some participants are angry that their high school did not give them what they anticipated and they feel let down by the experience. Nino, Peter and Stacey all felt that opportunities were lacking in their school. Nino believed she did not get to truly experience high school because of the newness of her school:

> There is a purpose to high school but I didn't get the full experience at my high school because I was part of an experiment to see if schools like mine would be beneficial to upcoming students. I did enjoy high school but I felt like I could of have had better opportunities in a school where I had more control over my classes.

Being a "part of an experiment" frustrated Nino, who has since rejected formal education. That frustration can play out in multiple ways. For Peter and Stacey, their frustration about the absence of clarity, the absence of opportunity and their having been part of an experiment provided the motivation to move forward:

> *Peter:* High school is a stasis, an incubator, a cocoon. High school is for you to learn yourself and what you want your future to be. It's the waiting room into real life. Take a number. I loved it and hated it. Loved it more.

> *Stacey:* In my high school we were all given support but not enough information, in my opinion. I learned more at my after school program than I did in my high school. So I had to do a lot of self research. I like my school but it needed a lot of help–granted, it was still new; '09 was the second graduating class. Not all the students were as motivated to go to college–I feel that my school failed them in that area.

While it is certainly important to have extracurricular activities and opportunities beyond the classroom, what does it say about the current state of school reform when there are few effective opportunities for college preparation *within* the walls of the school? New York City public school students do have access to college readiness programs, but these exist as adjuncts to regular school responsibilities, adding to the already heavy burden schools carry. Stacey's observation that all students were given support but not a lot of information is revealing: The students were provided a consistent environment but not one that genuinely readied them for life after high school. She acknowledges that not all students were motivated, which will happen irrespective of school or community resources, but without the unearned privilege of social capital, students without motivation are effectively ill prepared for life after high school.

(Ill-)Prepared for College

Because many of the participants believe that the purpose of high school is to prepare students for college or an independent life, I inquired whether they themselves felt prepared for college. The participants who graduated most recently were a bit nervous about their preparation while the older participants had two to three years of college to help them determine, in hindsight, if they had been satisfactorily prepared. Last, who graduated in 2008 and took a semester off before starting at a local community college, believes that high school "in its purest form" should prepare students for college and higher learning, yet, "ours did nothing of the sort and was more of a cesspool of personalities." This "cesspool of personalities" is part of the struggle with small start-up schools. Especially in New York City, start-up schools are challenged in their effort to build culture. Students travel from all over the city to attend school, so there is little opportunity for community connection. In part because small schools have limited budgets, there are fewer extracurricular options within the walls of the school, which troubled many of the participants. Yet the "cesspool of personalities" is also one of the benefits of small schools, where young people meet, interact with and become friends with people different from themselves. That small schools celebrate this diversity is important, but the celebration does not continue past high school. When these young people graduate from high school and start work or college, they enter a more complex environment that assumes people come from different environments. The school's emphasis on personal attention and personalities is something many of the participants speak of approvingly, and they reach that observation through a variety of methods and over the course of multiple struggles, often when they see it *not* celebrated in their current environments.

In June 2010, just after his high school graduation, Brick felt that he was partially prepared for college. He explains:

> As for the coursework I think a part of me is prepared for it but part of me is not. I don't feel really ready for the essays that I probably will have to do in college. We never really got many essays in 12th grade to prepare us for that. Also,

same with the tests. I mean I did pretty good on tests and I did study, but I feel the teachers gave us too many chances to fix our tests or gave us open note tests which didn't really require us to study. I just think they could have been harder during 12th grade. So I probably will have trouble with the tests at first 'til I get a handle of things and how to schedule everything.

Brick is a highly motivated student; during high school he would generally get his work done correctly and on time the first time, then refine it while less motivated classmates caught up. In this way, Brick was prepared for the rigors of college, though not for the necessary independence without reward. By October of his first year at college, Brick grappled with the course load and time management. He detailed:

> The semester so far is going okay. I'm having a hard time getting control over things and making a schedule. Classes are going pretty good–I have 3 classes: Computer Science, Fictional Techniques and From Alchemy to Chemistry. Really each class is considered two classes because for each one I have to do an independent study.

Brick felt mostly stressed by the amount of reading, explaining, "High school didn't prepare me for the reading that is required. It is really nerve wracking and hard to get a handle and keep up with everything. The workload is a lot more than in high school. But slowly getting everything settled." He finished his first year quite strongly and has developed solid relationships with his science professors, which will be discussed in Chapter Five. The independence needed in college is in direct opposition to the participants' high school experience where, as Brick explained, there was always extra time to do work, work could be regularly redone and tests were open-book or open-notes.

Popcorn, about to start his senior year in college, had an experience similar to Brick's. During his first semester in college he realized he was completely unprepared for the workload and made a significant change in his study habits. In May 2009, after completing his first year of college, he explained:

> I wasn't intellectually prepared for college. But I was driven. I knew what I had to do: I did my work, I set aside time to do it. I was always in the library, never slacked off. You know what I mean, it's putting in time. Because I had that drive, I quickly understood and got used to the routine and how classes are run and like stuff like that.

What many participants discovered when they left high school was how restricted their experience had been, and not all possessed the motivation or knowledge they needed to succeed.

In an effort to enable the success of all students, the work ethic at LSHS (typical of many small schools) was to permit students to continuously revise work until it was satisfactory. While this may teach valuable lessons about revision and editing, it minimizes the importance of time-management and deadlines. Less motivated students who knew there was revision time built into the deadlines would often put off any attempt to do the work until after the due date. Both Brick and Popcorn had the "drive," as Popcorn names it, to get the work done on time, which inevitably assisted their transition to college. But their drive could not overcome what their school lacked. Most troubling was the absence of core courses necessary for college admission.

While in high school Popcorn was very critical of the larger system of schooling, and after starting college he refined that criticism, condemning the shortcuts his high school took:

> The thing is, look, if the system knew that we didn't take Spanish, like a formal Spanish class, I would not be in college. But you know what? I am in college! And I'm loving it! And I didn't take Spanish. You know, what does that say? The system is weak. And the system needs to be fucking reexamined. I was lucky. You know what I mean, me and a couple other kids, we're lucky. But there's a lot of kids that aren't lucky.

There were no formal language options at LSHS, so students took a modified Spanish class for approximately 10 weeks each year. While this is a violation of New York City Department of Education standards, the sheer quantity of infractions in the larger school system means that this went unnoticed for several years. Students struggling with serious coursework in college start their university training at a disadvantage, in part because of infractions such as this. Participants had been told that the curriculum prepared them for the rigors of college, but upon entry to college (and without any other high school experience with which to compare), they realized they had been misinformed. Some students, as Popcorn explains, got "lucky," which is not an auspicious way to begin college.

In May 2009, a year after graduating, Bruce, who was fluctuating between a sociology or journalism major at his community college, felt that high school had prepared him for college. He explains, "In the sense of the workload yes, especially my senior year. It's like they were out to make me get in the habit of writing many pieces at a time," which he felt helped him with his journalism assignments. However, as will be shown in Chapter Five, Bruce has waffled in his attention to college. He forgot to register one semester and spent that time playing video games. He then refound his focus and re-registered the following semester as a communications major, changing the broader picture of what he wanted to do with his life. Bruce struggles with time management and did not make the same concerted effort to focus on his studies that Brick and Popcorn did. Though "they" (his teachers) worked to get him in the habit of writing, he did not participate fully in his part of the process.

Stacey, who graduated in 2009 and attends a private college on Long Island, believes that work she did outside of high school was more useful in preparing her for college than the work she did in her school. "I think because it was my early exposure to college life, like what to bring, life on campus." She enrolled in a program that invited high school students to participate in college classes and spend nights in the college's dorms, which she believes provided a thorough lesson on the whole college experience:

> It gives the students the going-away experience and shows that though they will be doing academics most of the time, they will still have fun. The early exposure helped me get a taste of what college life would be like. I believed that helped me see there is a time to play and a time to be serious. When no one is there to tell you that, you have to decide whether you're going to do the work.

Stacey also acknowledges she had great support from her mother, who lives in New York City less than an hour from campus, and her grandmother, who lives on Long Island near her school. When things got stressful, it was easy for Stacey to reach out to her family support immediately.

Genevieve, who graduated at the top of her class in 2009, struggled mightily during her first semester in college. Her complete story will be discussed in greater detail in Chapter Six, but in brief, she felt completely unprepared for college. When we spoke in January 2010, soon after she had returned home to New York City after failing out of school, she was hesitant to explain what had happened. She mostly blamed herself for poor study habits without taking into account the struggles inherent in moving away from home to a completely unfamiliar environment with no support system. In her first semester in college she struggled in a course called Biology of Sex, which she claims "is not as fun as it sounds." She then explains, echoing Brick and Popcorn, that at LSHS "you really don't have to have study habits in order to get good grades," which made the expectations of college a rude awakening:

> Coming to college, especially in this particular class, you had to study every night and it wasn't an hour and you're done with it, no, you had dedicate whole-heartedly to that class in order to understand and to pass those tests. I mean, at the beginning, I was up with all my classes. I was good. When you have classes every other day, that's when the procrastination kicks in, and it's like, okay, I have this to do, let me do this and then I'll study for that class tomorrow, I'll have plenty of time. And then that time, it goes.

By March 2010 Genevieve had enrolled in a local community college and was excelling in her classes and extracurricular activities. While the workload may be easier than at the private university, more importantly for Genevieve, she is in a familiar environment with familiar people as a support system. Her confidence to take intellectual and social risks grows with the stable support system in place. She had a new perspective on her struggles. She had heard that her high school was allowed to make up its own curriculum and did not have to follow the Department of Education standards. She believes that LSHS took too many risks. "It was a chance for them to sort of find different creative ways in order for us to understand the material that we need to learn, in order to graduate, in order to pass Regents[1] and stuff like that." While this is not the exact truth, it is understandable how Genevieve could come to believe this: The students were told they were in a unique education environment that did not have to follow the standards of "regular" schools. They were told they were allowed to do their own thing. Small schools did have greater curricular freedoms, especially with theme integration. They were not exempt from city and state requirements; instead, they were expected to achieve those requirements through alternative methods. This often works on a small scale in focused, dedicated classrooms (Ancess & Allen 2006; Tyner-Mullings 2008), yet it is prohibitively harder to replicate on a larger scale (Ravitch 2010). Genevieve associates the curricular struggles directly with the poverty experienced by most of her classmates. She believes that because she and most of her classmates were impoverished, the curriculum was "watered down." She explains:

> If you gave us just the basic curriculum, a system that was known to set us up to fail, then we all would have failed and we all wouldn't be looking to college and like outside of high school. We would just be looking for that 9–5 job, just getting all that money like that. I think they were just so afraid to challenge us that we wouldn't be interested anymore. I wish they just would have had more faith in us, in you know, in our intellect. Then we all would have been better off.

As part of the second graduating class of the high school, she saw many 2008 graduates return to visit the school, lamenting that they were unprepared for life after high school. She explains that during her senior year:

> Past seniors are coming to the school, cursing the teachers and cursing the principal and the school, like "You didn't prepare us! We failed! You didn't prepare us!" And I mean, we all had great times, great experiences, but when it comes down to this, we all wanted to go to college, we're sitting in the classroom, like, what is this? We never took tests every week, we didn't really have to worry about our studying habits, we had presentations where we could bullshit our way to pass.

She believes high school was too easy, in part because in working to make assignments creative and fun, the school ignored what would be expected of the students next. If high school is indeed a place for preparation, these young people were not adequately prepared. Genevieve explains:

They really focused on our personal styles, on presentations. I guess us kids couldn't afford private school or afford to go to a school that taught you that curriculum that would be matched up with college level and stuff like that. Our environment, that was also a disadvantage to us. We're low-income students.

The school encouraged and promoted college as a goal but college acceptance and matriculation do not guarantee success at coursework or the ability to balance new freedoms and increased responsibilities. What was not made clear was that college acceptance was the first of many goals, and that greater attention to schoolwork would be needed to stay afloat and ultimately graduate from college.

Pivotal Personal Moments: College

While some participants had life-altering experiences in high school, many experienced significant interpersonal and academic struggle early in their college careers, when they realized the depth, or dearth, of support in their lives. Pivotal moments in college also helped to further define their understandings of friendship.

After Genevieve's struggles in upstate New York she was embarrassed to return home "a failure" but soon realized how important it was to be near her friends and family. She explains, "I felt by me coming home, I would somehow feel far from them in success and in distance. But we still involve each other in our lives. No matter how much we have grown, we still sort of stayed the same." After returning home, Genevieve not only forged new friendships with classmates at community college, she also developed a stronger, more adult relationship with her mother and grandmother. She is a godmother to a friend's baby, a responsibility she takes very seriously. She believes that were it not for her struggles away from home, she would not be able to construct these "grown up" relationships. During her first term in college she rarely posted to Facebook, not wanting "friends" to know her struggles. Since returning to New York City, she posts regularly, sharing school and personal news, especially when she was the lead in the school play. While the majority of participants are regular Facebook users, what cannot be known is whether a break in posting means they are in crisis, overly committed to other responsibilities, or just lurking on the site. The absence of data on Facebook is itself data, though much more difficult to codify and organize.

In some cases, participants learned about severed relationships and how to maneuver past them. Stacey, who was raised along with her younger brother by her single mother, was contacted by her absentee father soon after her high school graduation. In May 2009 we had a long talk in which she expressed mixed feelings about re-establishing contact with the man who had made, at best, sporadic attempts to see her. Within a year, she had established a consumerist relationship with her father. In June 2010, she explained, "After getting in touch with my father, whatever I asked for he provided: A new iPod, a laptop and a new TV for my room next semester. But we really didn't bond or really get to know each other due to his lack of consistency. Even now since I have been home I have not heard from him in almost two months." By April 2011 she had disconnected from her father, explaining vaguely, "We are not speaking for awhile. He said some very hurtful things that can never be forgiven. Life was better off without knowing who he was." She sighs, "other than that things have been good." Like Genevieve, Stacey did not announce this development as an explicit change in status posed to her Facebook page. Because Facebook can be the ultimate inside joke, some more obscure status updates need cautious interpretation: Might they reveal a deeper truth about one's pain and struggle, or might they just be a momentary reaction? When Stacey posts "urrrghh" as a status update, is this cause for concern?

A particularly salient challenge for young people is the maintenance of friendship through hard times and growing pains. All throughout high school, Peter, Bruce and Popcorn were inseparable best friends. Together and as individuals, they were bright, spirited, kind young men. Personally, they were very important to me; Peter was one of the first students I met when I started working at LSHS and he introduced me to his friends. When I first began research for *Media Education Goes to School*, the group interviews I conducted with these young men were what set the tone for the text in its entirety. I sympathized with their nervousness about leaving each other for college, and when we spoke or met throughout the early college years, I always asked how the long-distance friendships were working for them.

For one year, Bruce and Peter attended the same community college; they were together while Popcorn left New York City to attend college. After their first year in college, this was something the young men were concerned about and were working through. Bruce remembers meeting Popcorn and Peter in high school, which was a pivotal moment of change for him. In the 9th grade Bruce experimented with being a "bad boy" and his relationship with Popcorn and Peter moved him past that phase. He explains, "After I grasped on to them, we grew, and they're like the only guys I speak to now, even after high school. Popcorn was away from home, but he wasn't that far. He's 45 minutes on the railroad," which to Bruce did not feel much longer than their commutes in high school when he and Peter lived in Brooklyn and Popcorn lived in Harlem:

> At first it was like, dag, Popcorn's leaving, he's going upstate. And with all the people talkin' about college, it's gonna be work, work, work, work, work, I'm not gonna see him 'til the holidays, so, it was kind of like, I'm gonna be here by myself. But me and Peter ended up going to the same school in the city so I've always had him, so it was just the thought of not seeing Popcorn.

Peter and Bruce visited Popcorn quite frequently, enough that they both made friends with Popcorn's college friends and were able to experience some "traditional" college parties. Popcorn even joked that Bruce knew more girls at his school than he did.

At the end of their first year in college, Peter received a scholarship to a traditional black college in the South. He had worked so hard at community college and improved his grades, while Bruce had been a bit lazy and worked less hard. The summer before Peter was to leave, Bruce was nervous about being alone, but was not nervous about the strength of the friendship. He explains:

> Through this five year relationship, goin' on six year relationship, we have been very strong. I feel as if three black males who connected and been friends for so long, we went through problems, but they weren't big, they weren't like life ending, they were just regular teenage problems and we just went over them. I have too much love and care for you as one of my brothers. So it's like, even if I don't speak to Popcorn for three months, I call him, it's still gonna be the same thing, 'cause it's like, he's one of my brothers. I feel more connected to Peter and Popcorn than my actual brothers. So even though it hurts that I can't call Peter and run to his house–'cause he used to live next to me, like a two minute bike ride to his house, and I sit there 'til like 4 o'clock in the morning and then go back home–that's gonna bother me, 'cause I know I'ma have them boring moments. But I just know when he comes back, or we'll video chat, it's just gonna be like, rejoice! And plus, it's not like he had to leave because of problems, he's leaving to succeed! So, it's like, when he comes back, it's like "How you doing?" and to catch up, so, it's always gonna be love, no matter what.

Unfortunately, this trust and admiration fell apart during the boys' sophomore year in college. When I met with Popcorn at the end of his sophomore year in college, he spoke a great deal about the importance of friendship. Popcorn had had a difficult year, which will be discussed in detail in Chapter Six, and he was disappointed in himself for losing focus. He felt that it was his faith in his friends that helped him regain his focus. He spoke less securely about his ability to stay in touch, even though they had had a successful year of visits. It was a while before he got to the crux of his anxiety:

> Friendships from high school, that's something I feel anxiety about because those are really significant friendships in who I am. These people really helped in molding who Popcorn is, and I don't want to lose these people. And I know what usually happens is, your high school friends, you're not really in contact with them as much anymore, so you lose those friendships and you see each other 20 years later and it's awkward. I don't want that to happen. That's the last thing I want to happen. I'm just trying to keep those friendships and those connections alive. It's really difficult.

Popcorn continued to grapple with his fears, talking about both personal and geographic change:

> The one thing that changed is–well, we all *changed*–we aren't really together as much anymore, we're dealing with way different people, our personalities expanded with time 'cause that's what happens. But, I feel like we all have that fear, that's what keeps us together because we know where we're all coming from, and where the core of our personalities are and we share that with each other.

He pauses, then clarifies that he does not believe *he* will lose his friends, and finally shares that he fears two of his friends have lost each other:

> We're always gonna be friends, but as of right now, we're not as close as we can be because, over the past year, conflict happened between Peter and Bruce. They're butting heads and then me, I want this to work–I want them to be friends. It's a really tense moment because Peter did something to Bruce that was really, really bad and Bruce is trying to get over that. Like he wants to, but he just can't. They haven't seen each other since Peter told him what happened.

Popcorn opts to not violate the boys' confidence and won't tell me what happened, but he held out hope for the summer. "This summer is basically dedicated to get back on the wagon and be like, be really good friends again. They just need to see each other and talk to each other and try to navigate how to get through it." Popcorn was in the awkward position of being confidante to both Peter and Bruce and hoping that his good spirits could bring them all together:

> I'm still good with both of them and, it's not so much choosing sides it's just wanting–it's a need–for there to be a wholeness again, like community again. What Peter did was wrong and we all acknowledged that and he knows and that's why he feels so shitty and Bruce knows and he wants to forgive him, but it's just not the type of thing that you can just forgive easily. In simple terms, it's fucked up what he did. But we all just want to get back to what we were.

Yet Popcorn is also aware that he needs to think about the changes he has been through and determine his own investment in maintaining two separate friendships. Peter kept his actions secret for almost a whole year, which made it harder for Bruce to forgive him. Because the wrongdoing was directly against Bruce, it was easier for Popcorn to forgive Peter. Though Bruce and Peter do not play out their conflict on Facebook, anyone who knows what happened might see subtle digital traces of the disagreement: Popcorn sends the same links, photos, videos or comments separately to Peter's and Bruce's pages, where he used to do group posts. Periodically, Popcorn posts pictures of all three of them from high school with captions such as "fam" or "I love these guys," possibly a subtle plea for Bruce and Peter to remember the strength of their bond.

In July 2010, I spoke with Bruce about the fight. Normally, Bruce is remarkably detailed in his discussion, hashing out minute details, but he was at best circumspect regarding Peter. He explains, "When people make decisions, once trust and respect, once you lose that from me, I don't put forth any effort. When someone makes a mistake, when someone's your friend and he does something, you brush it aside. Not the level of mistake he made."

One year later, in June 2011, though Peter will not discuss the details, he admits it was his error and he wishes Bruce could forgive him:

> I made my mistake and I did as I did and we don't talk anymore, but I still love him. That was my brother. We were like Bruce Wayne and Peter Parker, like freakin' superheroes! And I would do anything to get him back, but he has to get over his hate for me. I said my apologies and I tried to work through, but you know, some people need their time. And that's what he needs.

While he is upset, he believes that he and Bruce are still brothers; now they are brothers who fight. Because both young men are still in close contact with Popcorn, there remains a connection, which Peter hopes will ultimately bring him and Bruce back together:

> I laugh about this with Popcorn. He remains in close contact with Bruce and in close contact with me. That's like an actual family of brothers and sisters not talking. Okay, so they can like not talk for 15 years, but they will eventually make up. Because they're a family. And that's what we've formed. We've become really close. So, you know, say Popcorn gets married five years from now–wow that's creepy, knowing that's a possibility in my life! You know, I go to the wedding and Bruce is gonna be there. We can't *not* exchange words, so, you know, we will eventually make up.

Until then, Facebook enables them to continue to monitor each other's progress and development from a digital distance. While they are no longer Facebook friends, they have so many mutual digital friends in common that each has relatively easy access to the other's site. Bruce spent much of the summer posting photos of jokes printed on popsicle sticks, which admittedly does not give profound insight into his life, but does show that he is around.

However, it must be remembered that Facebook posts hide as much as they reveal: In posting so many jokes, is Bruce hiding deeper fears about his progression and growth? Facebook enables users to constantly share personal information, but it is also worth considering whether Facebook can be a place to garner greater civic participation.[2] In the constant updating of information on Facebook there is a corresponding noise, and this noise makes it more challenging to tease apart personal updates from larger civic issues. Most participants use Facebook for personal reasons, yet as they grow into adulthood, they become more aware of their larger world and its challenges beyond their immediate environment.

Larger World and Political Issues

While the participants learn a lot from their interpersonal connections, the majority claim they do not pay attention to civic, activist or political issues. At best, some pay attention to issues they find personally important, but most acknowledge that politics and world issues are not topics that interest them. While most claim they do not pay attention, they all can cite multiple current events. One might assume that because the mission of their high school is to use the media to foster social change, these young people might be more critically informed, but as shown in Chapters Two and Three, they do not display formal critical analytic skills. Simply knowing *about* larger world news substitutes for analysis and direct involvement.

Many of the participants claim they only pay attention to larger world issues if it is something that directly affects or interests them:

Genevieve: I have to be honest and say that I don't pay too much attention to politics. I've never been interested in them unless an issue that deeply affects me catches my attention, then I would follow it.

Hass: I keep up with politics only when it has to do with New York issues or when it has to do with foreign issues.

Jacline: I don't pay attention to politics except when it's something that directly affects me or I'm interested in. I don't follow it unless it grabs my attention. Because I feel it is too complicated and that their sole purpose should be the needs of the people and sometimes it feels like that is not the case.

Larger issues only matter if, as Jacline and Genevieve phrase it, they are "something that directly affects me." While Hass is less precise–New York or foreign issues are both broad categories–he similarly speaks about things that affect him: local New York City issues or information from his home country, Colombia, where his grandparents live.

The participants who do pay attention do so with trepidation because they feel they are being lied to, or because there is no impact on their lives:

Helena: I don't really like it. I think it's important to know who and what is dealing with our country and the world's issues but I don't like it because I don't feel like it is the 100% truth at all.

Natalie: I pay very little attention to politics. I did take a class in politics but I just didn't have the time I desired to study it in depth. It is very complicated to keep track of and there so many things that go on and nobody really pays attention to it.

Nino: I do pay attention to politics, but it just infuriates me that I have to rely on complete strangers who have their own motives for their usage of the power given to them.

Helena, Natalie and Nino reveal the challenge in paying attention to larger world issues: How to choose what to pay attention to. This can be a daunting task, especially in a global city such as New York. Many participants have families in other countries and try to pay attention to local news in those countries as well. However, some participants are mostly uninterested, seeing little to no relevance in political issues:

Jasmine: I don't really follow politics too much unless it's the presidential elections.

Johnny: I don't really understand how politics affect my life.

Peter: I don't care about politics, but it does intrigue me. I tend to listen from time to time and if not engage in debates, then take part in a voyeuristic sense. I care about life.

Some participants try to increase their attention to larger world issues and attempt an interest in politics as they see themselves becoming independent, autonomous adults:

Brick: I do pay attention to some politics. It isn't as interesting to me but after 12th grade I have gotten a bit more interested in what is going on around the world and our country. It has just started to interest me because I have a say and if I want something done then I must know what is going on around the world and so I can spread my ideas and get others aware of what is happening. I feel what is important to me is the wars that are going on and how the USA is dealing with the national debt.

John: I used to not, but now I do. It's hard to keep up, there are so many things and ideas talked about but it's best to be aware. I watch the news; It saddens me but I'd rather be well informed. I become angered by the violence, ignorance, stupidity and abuse of power in the world and of things that happen in countries like Iran and whatnot.

Snapper: I pay attention to politics most of the time. Not everything happening in the world has to concern me unless I'm in danger, so I've been paying less attention lately. I have been concerned with a lot of the decisions being made though. I think as Americans, we have a huge role in countries all around the world, but we have a lot of problems of our own as well.

Pink: When it comes to politics at times I do pay mind to it because I want to know what they're offering us and what are their views of the economy because the economy is real bad right know. Even though I feel politicians will just tell you what you want to hear to get things their way.

Brick, John, Snapper and Pink all know there are issues that are important to be informed about, and Brick says that his right to have a say means he has a responsibility to pay attention. Snapper acknowledges that "danger" is a motivating factor to paying attention to things beyond his own personal sphere. The belief that politicians lie is echoed by Pink.

Despite not paying attention to politics or larger world issues, most of the participants can name current events in the news:

John: The issues are many, but global warming, oil and trying to find alternative energy sources, the ongoing wars, ongoing racism and abuse of power, Iran, Middle East, China, lack of freedom of speech and of course, the ongoing violence in Africa. I can go on.

Jasmine: I believe that the most important issues are providing children the best education and global warming. Education has become a big issue because public schools haven't been able to receive enough funds to offer different academic programs, such as tutoring, SAT and Regents prep, and afterschool programs. These types of programs are sufficient in helping students to excel in school. Global warming is a long-running issue that will affect the outcome of the future. The world would need to build strong communities who can contribute to preventing global warming with numerous strategies, such as recycling, conserving energy, and planting more gardens and grass fields. These issues impact my future because I think about the sake of my future children and worry about if they will be able to fulfill their goals in the college of their dreams. If global warming continues at this rate, my future is at risk.

Genevieve: The most important issues to me are dealing with the environment. Our dependence on oil has given us more loss and grief than convenience and happiness. Gay rights involving legalizing marriage, the government's involvement in, or lack of, our economy are some issues that I also care a lot about.

Hass: One important issue I would say is global warming.

Jacline: The most important issues in the world right now to me are climate control and pollution, hunger and poverty, and war and terrorism.

Snapper: I also believe our debt is another big issue. It's been growing like crazy lately, and it seems like nobody's ready to start fixing it yet until things get really bad.

In an era of 24–hour cable news channels and constant Facebook updates, there is a lot of data at their disposal. They can know a lot–quite quickly–by paying only the most superficial attention. News comes at them more and more quickly but not necessarily with more thorough treatment. Current events can move past them without provoking much attention.

For the most part, participants touch upon some of the most salient issues of our time, but they do not include themselves in the experience. Only Jasmine speaks about educational issues in a general sense; separately, all speak about their own educational dilemmas. They see their troubles as wholly personal, not as part of a larger matrix of which they are a part. That something is labeled "politics" means it is removed from their immediate realm. In this way, young people are lulled into believing these subjects have little to do with them. Even when the participants discuss continued struggles with the economy, the debt crisis, or wars being fought on multiple fronts, they do not see how their own participation matters. Their own financial difficulties are somehow separate from the larger discussion of the economy.

Only Natalie, Pink and Lucy connect their personal experiences with larger political stories:

> *Natalie:* An important issue that is going on in America now is immigration. Recently the Arizona bill was passed in which immigrants (mostly Latinos) were going to have to identify their alien status to any police officer who asked. Mostly Mexican and people of Hispanic descent were going to be asked because it was reported in the news that a police officer wouldn't stop a blue-eyed, blonde European. I just hate that they stereotype the word *immigrant* with a caramel skin, black-haired person.

As a Latina with a largely immigrant family, including family members who have been stopped by police for not being "blue-eyed, blonde Europeans," Natalie connects the struggles in Arizona with her own experiences. Making this connection shows Natalie she is a part of, not apart from, politics.

Pink sees her position as a lesbian represented in issues of marriage equality rights and opposition to Don't Ask, Don't Tell, prior to its repeal:

> The most important issues in the world to me are gay marriage, the war and the economy. Gay marriage should be legal, there's so many other things in the world going on, people are dying because of poverty, the wars that seem never ending, but yet they seem to be more concerned about who I want to marry. In the war, our soldiers are dying, innocent people are being attacked. I also disagree with the Don't Ask, Don't Tell policy; there are people fighting, putting their life at risk and they can't be themselves. Their sexual orientation shouldn't matter–what should matter is the fact that they're fighting for this country.

Pink's observation that "they seem to be more concerned with who I want to marry" puts those larger issues into perspective: While the world appears to be falling apart, marriage equality becomes a convenient smokescreen to distract citizens from larger issues. With this observation, Pink unveils one of the greatest triumphs of neoliberalism: The ability to sneak in and rearrange institutions while average citizens are busy paying attention elsewhere (Harvey 2010; Klein 2007).

Lucy's sarcasm reveals an awareness of and frustration with the state of the world. "I worry from watching *2012*. I don't want to die yet. Nah, seriously–I do worry about this recession, and worry that Obama doesn't have the experience to get us back on track. So far–no good Obama. But nah, I ain't really a fan of the news and newspapers, I go straight to the sports section." Though she quips about the fears of apocalypse in 2012–referencing the apocalyptic disaster film *2012* (Emmerich 2009)–she also speaks of a deeper concern about the recession. Lucy chose not to attend college because she does not like school and needs to make money to pay her bills in order to remain independent, and in the continued tailspin of the recession, she has difficulty doing this. Going "straight to the sports section" invites a willful catharsis. Brick, John, Snapper and Pink all acknowledged that paying attention to politics becomes important as they become adults, which led me to wonder if the participants felt more or less like adults after high school.

Growing up After High School

As all of the participants have now moved out of high school and into college or work, I was curious whether they felt they had "grown up." The most recent graduates feel that they grew up a lot while in high school, and see high school graduation as the culmination of certain learning as they prepare to learn more:

> *Brick:* I can't say I feel like I have grown up since graduating high school seeing as I just graduated. I can say that from the beginning of high school to graduation I have grown up a lot. I feel more like I can stand on my own two feet in the world now.

> *John:* To be frank, yes and no. Graduating is very significant to me, and it symbolizes a change in mentality. I know I need to grow up and take on adult roles: Work, bills, living. To be honest, I'm scared, I want to do something with my life, become something I can be proud of and that I can someday help others.

The participants are all within the frame Arnett (2004) names "emerging adulthood." Many of the participants, especially those paying for college on their own, and those who have forgone college to go directly to work, have significant adult responsibilities, yet believe themselves to be in an in-between, relatively unstable place, especially as they relinquish some of the irresponsibility of childhood as it is (voluntarily or forcibly) replaced by real-world responsibilities.

Real-world responsibilities can be a source of stress for young people, as Johnny and Last indicate. Johnny especially appears to be caught up in his instability and knows he needs to take more responsibility for his actions and choices, claiming, "the most important thing I've learned in life is you have to work for everything you want. There are no freebies." Last, who struggled to complete high school, now wants to be more proactive in his choices, to see that there are "no freebies" as Johnny phrases it, and to accept this as a motivator, stating, "I haven't grown up. I've grown out. I'm the same person I was, maybe even a younger person. I do believe though that I am more ready to accept challenges when they aren't given to me directly."

The older participants who attend college situate their growth within the environment of school:

Jasmine: Attending college, I meet many individuals from all over the world and they have taught me important life values. Partaking in college courses and living in a college dorm have allowed me to become more outgoing and mature to college professors and students. I enjoy participating in various clubs and organizations because I find my self-identity with the activities I partake in and the people I meet. I have overcome many hardships and challenges to move on in life for the better.

Natalie: I feel like I have grown up since high school because college hit me hard with the workload. I take life a little more seriously looking at every person I meet as a networking possibility.

Snapper: I think I've matured since I graduated high school. I've spent a year on my own managing myself and living on my own, so I pretty much had to get used to fending for myself. I also matured mentally. I see things around me a lot differently than I would have four years ago.

College provided a further step to independent living while also providing a space for intellectual risk-taking and exploration. Similar to Lucy, who connected high school with the bravery needed to come out as a lesbian, Jasmine, Natalie and Snapper see their maturity and growth enabled by their university experiences.

Participants such as Lucy and Pink, who went from high school directly to work, attribute their growth to very practical lessons:

Lucy: Yes I feel like I've grown. For starters I don't live with my mom, I don't depend on anyone's pocket but mine and I have a mind of my own. I quit EVERYTHING (which is very important to me) and my mentality has completely changed. If it weren't for that trip to Cali' I would have been a pothead living with my mom, no job and broke.

Pink: After graduating from high school I don't necessarily feel "grown up," but I do feel like I have more responsibilities. I have to manage work, to move out, and attend college. I guess in a way I have "grown up" because those are my responsibilities now, no longer my parents'.

To grow up after high school is to face the realities of work and college. While college can delay work and adult responsibilities for four more years, all the participants in this study have significant real world knowledge beyond the walls of any school environment. Stacey sums up succinctly what they have all learned: "I don't feel grown up but I do have more freedom and a lot more responsibility now. There is no one to do things for you—it is all up to you." Chapter Five draws from this crux of freedom and responsibility as it meets independence to explore how the participants make meaning of college and work.

FIVE

"I'm Size Medium": The Transition to Work and College

As Popcorn, a young African American man, prepares for his junior year in college in August 2010 he knows he is no longer a boy but does not quite feel like an adult yet. Thinking about where is he, he muses:

> Well I feel like I'm not a boy. And I'm not a man. I would say I'm a young man. Like, the young men's section...I'm size medium. I feel like I'm in this in-between phase, I'm only 19, I don't have a job and I'm not paying my own bills, you know what I mean, I'm not handling real world problems yet. You know, it's still school, you know I got a C in class, you know what I mean, those problems, they're only so big, but I feel I'm a young man. I'm like growing into that.

For young people choosing academic or career paths, the moments of transition are revelatory. Popcorn is an emerging adult (Arnett 2004), not yet solely responsible for his development, who is able to explore his interests as a full-time college student. Popcorn was successful in his first year of college; he admits he lost his way in his sophomore year and knew he needed to be focused in his junior and senior year, especially when he studied abroad in Paris.

This chapter explores how young people make meaning of the points of transition in their lives and their reflections on how those moments will frame their educations and careers. Many of the participants who left home and New York City for college have returned: The journey away was fraught with too many difficulties and they felt more secure, more able to take intellectual risks, when they were in familiar territory or within close reach of family and deep-depth friends. The participants who are further through college have also had their foundations challenged on personal levels: The post-high school years saw disruptions to friendships, intimate relationships and family bonds heretofore thought secure. Many of the participants who feel they are not "college material" have chosen work or the military, believing them to be sources of security. Yet, those who have made these choices have not found the security they anticipated and continue to struggle.

Young people with a wealth of social capital are often encouraged to take a "gap year" (Williams 2008) in order to find themselves or construct themselves into more competitive actors worthy of elite university attention. For young people with a dearth of social capital, a gap year might be too risky and might serve to set them back too far to be competitive. Especially in times of continued economic crisis, the pressure to make binding choices may be detrimental. Some participants have made potentially destructive choices: Bruce has "temporarily" left school because he forgot to register on time. Lucy, who struggled with drugs and alcohol in high school, then cleaned up for about a year, recently decided that the "high life" was more fun. Hass, who graduated from high school in 2010, planned to join the military because he believed he would make more money and would not have to "waste more time" at school, yet he has yet to meet with a recruiter. This chapter focuses on that brief period between high school and college or work to illustrate how those in precarious social and economic positions make choices that they believe will provide them security but in fact adhere them more firmly to social and economic servitude.

Life Between High School and College

For high school graduates, the time between high school and college can be an exciting if uncertain time. Those with plans for college have but a few months to prepare and to spend time with their high school friends before a major change. For those with no concrete plans, it can be a vague, ill-defined time. Some use the time productively; others develop a pattern of work and socializing that might restrict them from moving forward. In any case, it is a challenging time for all graduates.

Hass spent the summer after graduation working at his middle school assisting his former principal in various administrative tasks. He claimed the salary was good and he worked only until 1 p.m., so as long as he got all his work done, so he was free all afternoon to spend time with his girlfriend. Other than that, he was "waiting 'til March to leave for boot camp. My family finally supports me going to the military. I sat them down and told them there's nothing that is going to change my mind about joining the Marines. Lately I've been working out, so when I leave at least I'll be fit." A year later, Hass still was waiting to leave for the Marines and spending most of his time with his girlfriend. He regularly gets teased on Facebook for being "cuffed," that is, attached to his girlfriend as if by handcuffs, but he enjoys his time with her and is not bothered by the teasing. He believes that those who tease him are just jealous.

John, who desperately wants to attend college but does not have the money or the appropriate documentation, still works at his uncle's bodega. In fall 2010, when many of his high schools friends were at college, he was feeling lonely but trying to focus on the positive. "Things were all school, school, school for me and now it's about working and family and focusing on myself. I am working every day except Mondays and Monday through Friday I pick up my nieces from school and take care of them and clean the house–basically I'm like a nanny in a way!" The time away from school and a deeper awareness of his personal struggles caused John, already an excitable young man, some serious anxiety:

> I realize I am super scared about my future. I keep pondering if I will be skilled enough to acquire a professional job or graduate from college. With my situation it has become difficult to attend school. My hopes are on this Dream Act and I grow desperate and impatient each and every day wondering how things will turn out for me. I want to attend college and become something great but there is so much fear.

John planned to work through December 2010, then see if he could make a change. Sadly, the Dream Act did not pass (Herszenhorn 2010), and he remained nervous about attending college. He had pinned a great deal of hope on the Dream Act because he felt he fit the criteria perfectly: He moved to the United States as a child, has no criminal record and desperately wants to attend college. In April 2011 John was still working at the bodega and taking care of his nieces:

> I have been very busy even without going to school. I have been stuck in a cycle: I'm working six days a week, twice on Sundays, and five days a week I'm a nanny babysitting my two nieces. This is repeated always, and it's quite the boring cycle and I barely have a social life as a result. Lucky for me there is Facebook and the Internet and my favorite, Netflix. I pass the time using these things whenever I become bored.

John also claims he has used the time to think about his future and what he wants to do with his life:

> Of course I have also taken the time to really think about my future and trying to fix my situation, what I wanna pursue in life, having a plan B. I'm young, but it's something I feel I need to do. Time is so valuable. I might return to school in the fall, not 100% sure yet. I'm at a standstill in life right now.

John appears to be available on Facebook all day long; he regularly posts his reviews of TV shows and films, links to top news sites and inspirational quotes or passages. On his birthday he made a promise to respond to every single well-wisher, and on the day after his birthday he posted that he had been successful: 100 birthday wishes via Facebook, 100 responses. The work he does for his uncle at the bodega and with his nieces clearly affords him the time to be online consistently; however, he acknowledges a certain fatigue with the "cycle" in which he has found himself.

Some of the participants took time off before college, time that was ill defined and did not facilitate focus. Last, the young man who struggled through high school, took some time to focus but not as much time as he wanted–a period that he refers to as "vacation": "I took six months off that I intended to be a year. My mom honestly would not stop nagging me and I ended up cutting my vacation in half." Some participants found during their time off what they really needed to be doing. Natalie took a year in order to work but realized that career prospects with just a high school diploma would afford little professional development. "I was unsure of going to college but due to my economic circumstance I knew it was a MUST. After that year I enrolled in community college. And now I am working and attending school fulltime." Natalie works at a supermarket, a job that does not interest her but does pay the bills and reminds her where she does not want to be. Pink, who struggled in high school and dropped out for over a year before re-enrolling at a different school, ultimately wants to attend law school, so she needs to make some money and choose a local undergraduate program first. "Since graduation, I've just been working. My plan is to study law, but first I need college. After LSHS I didn't attend school, I struggled finding a school that would take me with the credits I had." Because she had missed so much school and had dropped out as a 16–year-old ninth grader, she was not a positive candidate for a traditional high school program. However, she met with a principal of a large school in Lower Manhattan who told her, "'I'll help you but you have to want to help yourself.' We both agreed that if she took me in, I would be focused on my work and I was, I ended up graduating from there in 2010." These interrupted periods ultimately can be valuable experiences, but while they are lived, they can feel extremely unstable.

Some participants started off lost and made positive changes in their time after high school. Lucy, a heavy drug user in high school, used her time after school to get cleaned up. The day before I left New York City, I ran into Lucy on the street. We were terribly excited to see each other–she, in part, because she had quit smoking pot and wanted to make sure I included that in her narrative. She was proud to have been a participant in *Media Education Goes to School* and wanted to be a part of this current research as a way of telling her new, sober story. She explained, "I quit smoking–a year ago to be exact–I'm not the dumb kid that you spoke to, I'm the hard-working 18–year-old who lives on her own now." Lucy later explained that quitting drugs was not her intention, but she was glad when it happened:

> I stopped smoking because I was forced to! After I graduated I was still smoking heavily and my mom couldn't take it. I was getting stopped by the police and it was getting worse. A week after the cops stopped me in front of my friend's building, my mom called me on my phone and told me she had a ticket to California, that it was time to change. I didn't know anyone, I was going to be living on a Marine base so I couldn't get high if I wanted to. And me and Diamond had got back together after a break we took and, well you know how she feels toward smokers.

A constant source of strife in their relationship was Lucy's drug use, of which Diamond did not approve. Lucy left for California where she lived with a cousin and her husband, who is in the Marines. She thought about joining the military, under her cousin-in-law's guidance, knowing the discipline would be good for her but ultimately chose not to:

> I was going to join the Air Force; he was going to school me on how the military worked but that didn't happen. I thought and thought hard–plus my girlfriend didn't want me to–and I decided I don't love America enough to die for it. Plus they don't accept who I really am, you know, since I'm gay.

Lucy moved back to New York and got an apartment with her girlfriend. For awhile things were going well; she got two part-time jobs, and she and Diamond opened a Facebook account together. "I got my girlfriend's name tattooed on my forearm and more to come. Me and Diamond, together for three years going on four." When I asked why they did not have separate Facebook accounts, Lucy laughed and said because Diamond did not trust her, which proved prescient. Early in the fall, Lucy and Diamond each established their own Facebook page and the two had a very public breakup on the site: Lucy had cheated on Diamond with another woman, with whom she was now living, and had started doing drugs again. Lucy soon paid more sporadic attention to Facebook, popping up to share her renewed interest in drugs and photos of her "son," a puppy she and her girlfriend adopted.

The Start of College: A Struggle

The participants who attended college right out of high school did not necessarily have an easier time adjusting to life after high school, even with the guidance that college offered. Many struggled to find their way, some adjusted quickly and others are still flailing.

Bruce started community college immediately out of high school and had difficulty finding his focus his first year. In May of 2009, at the end of his first year in college, he explained:

> I'm in a community college in New York. I kind of blame my high school for me being still here. But then I evaluated other students' progression after high school, and I matured and I came to my senses that it's my fault that I'm in community college. Given the circumstances with my family's finances, I'm better off in the city for right now until I can get my grades up and apply for scholarships. In high school, I would have to say, my work ethic was never there. So, I got through my first year in college and now going into my second year, I know what I gotta do. The only thing I'm worried about is finances for books. I'm ready to start the second year of college.

Upon reflection, Bruce blamed his high school because it did not seem to have an established routine to help students through the process. Though he once thought his high school had prepared him well, with time to reflect, his perspective shifted. He explained, "It was brand new, so they molded the high school around me and my peers, the first graduating class. They didn't have things established, they didn't have any seniors for us to learn from." This represents a struggle in school reform: The excitement and promise of starting a new school does not necessarily translate to successfully running the school, especially when the first graduating class has no one to look up to or learn from in the process. Bruce's experience matches what much of the literature says about start-up and charter schools and the challenges they face.[1] In addition, for students who are the first in their families to attend college (if not the first in their family to graduate from high school), the months and years after high school can be frustrating.

After his second year in college, Bruce changed his mind and decided to be a communications major with a focus on journalism. He decided to get to know as many people as possible to network his skills, and was eager to develop his writing, working with a "real journalist," one of his professors who also wrote professionally. By his second year in college he had learned that "no one cares if you have things to do; if you don't do them then it's your own responsibility." Bruce, who was coddled through high school, was now on his own. His two best friends had left town and he was relatively alone in Brooklyn, keeping in touch with his friends via long distance. He and Peter got into their fight and Bruce faltered in school. He missed the 2010 fall semester "due to laziness. I registered late and due to the fact that my school is over capacity a lot of classes were taken up. I plan on going back in January." He once again changed his major, moving away from journalism to study communications more broadly so he could, in his words, "have an umbrella effect of careers to choose." He was planning to leave his job at a trendy watch store in order to work at a clothing store where the pay was a bit better and the merchandise more varied.

By May 2011 he had returned to school and left once again. He was quick to point out that he had not failed out rather, he was "flaking" because "being in school confuses me; I don't have any clarity on what I want to do and also I'm in debt. So I am not in school this semester, but I have a headstrong start on something I am very interested in." He developed an interest in entertainment marketing and got an internship at a New York City-based public relations firm. He does administrative work for the company, which has taught him the language of marketing and public relations. "I help manage a street team which consists of putting together monthly and weekly schedules, mailings, and organizing flyers for reps. I also do press sweeps for events we do. I've hosted an event, and also help manage street teams outside of New York City. I get paid here and there and also get to attend concerts for free." While it does not sound like steady work–he only gets paid "here and there"–it does appear that Bruce finds some clarity in this role. His admitted lack of focus and debt may be just enough to keep him away from school for the foreseeable future; Bruce does not have the luxury of a "gap year" (Williams 2008), yet he works to carve some sort of plan for himself.

Like Bruce, Peter had a couple years of struggle before settling into a more productive routine. Peter attended the same community college as Bruce for his first year, and he did so well that he received a scholarship to a traditional black college in the South. He was so excited that he did not realize at first that the scholarship was only partial, and the stress of having to find the remainder of his tuition made his first semester away from home difficult. Like Bruce, Peter maneuvered his way through high school on his charm and good cheer. Even when he did not do his homework or stay focused in class, it was hard for teachers to discipline him, and ultimately he would get the work done. He made it through high school with few negative consequences. When attending the competitive college, he learned the hard way that such behavior would no longer work for him. After his first year away, he explains, "College is all about you–you do what's best for you. No one will 'advise' you to do anything. If you have problems at home you leave it home, coming to class with an attitude will do nothing for you. High school they send you to a counselor. College they send you to the registrar to drop the class." His struggles, he says, were a "long story" involving lack of funds, inattention to the expectations of his courses and anger at the people he felt had misled him:

> I came here with a 3.8 GPA and was told I had a scholarship. Then I got here and they told me I did not have a scholarship and I had to follow up. And I've never heard anything like that, that you have to follow up on something you've been rewarded with, and even so I constantly kept calling the school back and forth the entire summer just to make sure that this was a scholarship or not. So I

got here and because of that I had to take loans and pay out of pocket and I was extremely depressed about that, extremely upset that the school offered me no financial assistance for having a 3.8 GPA and I didn't do anything my first two semesters here. I only passed two classes. Two. So the school removed me. So over the summer I took a class in the city. And then I had to take classes during the fall semester in New York. And that brought me back here. And now I have three Bs and a C.

The 3.8 GPA at community college was exemplary, and evidence that he was capable of college-level work, but at a competitive private college, it was just on par with the majority of students. For the first time he could remember, Peter was alone and unable to charm his way out of a crisis; he no longer felt special. He toyed with the idea of joining the Coast Guard because he figured he could make money while they paid for his tuition but decided against it, believing the military was no route to success for a black man from New York City; he felt he would just be another body, not somebody special.

Some of the other participants faced similar difficulties during their first year in college and made dramatic–sometimes, frightening–changes. Jacline initially attended a small private college in upstate New York. While still a senior in high school, she was excited by the opportunity, but early in her first year away, she was faltering. She explains:

I got sick when I went away. I am asthmatic and I didn't prepare myself for the weather and while there I thought I could deal with it. I didn't take care of myself the way I should have and thought I would take two days of bed rest on my own and it was a few weeks before finals, so I was backed up on work. Trying to catch up was hard because of the amount of work and because it was my first time doing this and especially alone in a new place without knowing what help to take advantage of and what I should do in similar situations. I did what I could and after the semester was over my parents told me I could come back home and transfer to a school close by and I did. I transferred and I have been learning what it means to be a college student, my grades improved and I learned things like how to talk to my professors to see how they can help me when I have questions and or concerns. Also that first semester away taught me a lot about college life so now I am doing extremely well, my GPA went from a little under a 2.0 to a 3.6.

Serenity shared an experience similar to Jacline's:

For my first year and a half I went to a school in South Carolina, on a full academic scholarship. However I didn't really like it–there was too much space and it was very hard to get around because I don't drive, and didn't have a car. I was so used to public transportation! I had to get outta there!

The experience of being away from the city was too much for Serenity, she was not able to adjust to the "too much space." Despite the environmental space of the campus, the school's residential space was minimal, and a series of catastrophes showed Serenity she no longer wanted to attend that school:

> It was really stressful. The school had me living in a hotel my sophomore year because the campus was overcrowded with freshmen and they accepted too many kids. There was talk about the school losing its accreditation, it was all over the news because the president started stealing money. Just pure foolishness, that wasn't worth me stressing out over.

Serenity had a cousin who attended a small public school she really enjoyed located outside Baltimore, Maryland, so Serenity looked into transferring. Because it was a public school and she had family nearby, she qualified for in-state tuition, and the commute would be easier to New York City, where her grandparents, guardian and twin brother lived. She is happy in Baltimore; after her first semester she explained to me, "I like it much better. It's pretty cool–now I have two years down and two more to go." She works multiple jobs while in school and has learned to balance her freedom with her responsibilities. "It's different from high school because we are more free in the dorms–you can go to class whenever you want, and have no one watching over you. It's your responsibility to do what you have to." The urban environment is also more familiar; though she argues that Baltimore's public transportation pales in comparison to New York City's vast system, she is able to travel to and from school and work with little difficulty.

Financial struggles are a genuine concern, even at community colleges where tuition is significantly less expensive than at private or four-year public schools. Even if Bruce had been focused on his courses, the financial strain was a continuous deterrent which may help explain his comment that he was "confused" by college. Planet J attends a local community college and because he has to pay for it himself, he attends only sporadically. He graduated from high school in 2008 and enrolled in college immediately but has not taken a full, uninterrupted year of courses. He explains, "I have been paying for my attendance out of my own pockets. Due to me skipping every other semester in order to pay the tuition bill, my graduation is delayed."

Some of the participants began college only to learn that it was not something they were interested in or able to pay the requisite attention. Johnny works two jobs instead of attending college in part because he did not focus during his two attempts at school. "Since I graduated high school I went to college in the fall of 2008 and got academically dismissed after three semesters." Johnny then enrolled in a special program at a local community college that provided intensive counseling and academic advising to students who had had difficulty in traditional college environments but he stopped attending that as well. Now he works two jobs that provide him enough money to maintain his social life, though not enough to save money. He is currently looking for a third job to ease financial strain.

Settling in: Enjoying College

While many of the participants struggled during their first semester or first year of college, a couple made a very smooth transition. Jasmine moved about four hours north of the city to attend a private school and met with immediate success and enjoyment; she was intrigued by the people she met and the variety of different things to which she was exposed:

> College is very different from high school. There are more people who have different interests in what they want to do in the future. Since college has a bigger student population than high school, you will have the chance to meet new friends more frequently and become involved in various school events and organizations. In high school, you can build closer relationships with friends and teachers. College offers many courses where most of the students can have the liberty of choosing out of their own interests. Most of the college courses are situated in lecture halls where it is difficult to participate in class and you must schedule an appointment during office hours to meet with a professor whereas in high school, students are motivated to interact in class and can conveniently meet with their teacher during class hours.

Jasmine majors in hospitality management and marketing and spent the first semester of her junior year traveling abroad as part of an international hospitality program in which students visit different hotels and kitchens to see how the work is done. She posted photos from her adventures to Facebook and regularly exclaimed how much fun she was having and how much she was learning.

Snapper, who graduated in 2009, moved about five hours north of the city to attend a state school. He initially was overwhelmed by the change in environment, in awe of the size of the campus and dorm life. He realized quickly that he would have to change his work habits. "The work may not be all that different, but you're held accountable for everything. You're given a lot less leeway and you're paying for everything too. The pressure can get to you but after your first year it's manageable." This echoes a fair number of comments from most of the participants. Because they always were allowed to redo their work in high school and there were few if any consequences if they did not complete work on time, the accountability exacted by college seemed very demanding. However, some of them are intrigued by the challenge and excited to learn about a new place. Snapper explains:

> I was so eager to go to a college so far from a place I've been used to for so many years that I just settled right in as soon as I got there. For the first few weeks it was hard though. I was getting used to the area and I didn't know anybody with

a car yet, so I ended up walking most of the time when I needed stuff. Being from the city I wasn't used to living somewhere so pedestrian-unfriendly so I had to do a couple of unusual things to get places until I got used to it.

Unfortunately, because of financial instability, Snapper has left his state university and now attends a vocational school in New York City. He enjoys it and is able to focus specifically on transportation engineering, his particular interest.

After some initial struggles, some participants found great happiness and success at their schools. After a difficult and lonely first semester, Brick found his stride in school and ended the year on a strong note. Just before the end of his first year, we were in touch while he was studying for finals:

School has been going pretty well. I have made a lot of progress in getting used to college. It definitely was not an easy transition but it has gotten easier over time. I will definitely be going into science and next year I will be hopefully working with my professor in his lab a couple hours a week and getting used to the lab and all that. Not sure what I really want to do in science, most likely chemistry or biology, but the professor I will be working with is a chemistry teacher, so I will get the chemistry aspect of things. I am excited for next year. I definitely will not be transferring schools.

Sometimes switching schools is the correct decision. Jacline, Serenity, Snapper and Genevieve all changed schools and in so doing, grew happier, healthier and more productive. After a few months back in New York City and enrolled in an architecture program at a local college, Jacline felt much more confident about her experiences:

The semester started great! I was accepted into the architecture program and I have been doing really well since I've been here. I really like it and I like what I'm doing and what I'm learning. My other classes are good as well. It's a lot of work now that I'm doing work in my particular field of interest but it's fun and the hard work is worth it and it's nothing I can't handle.

She was happy to be home with her family, especially her sisters, with whom she is very close.

Serenity, who has lived most of her life in transition, saw her change of colleges as just another transition to manage. "I've always been independent and basically raised myself. So going away to college wasn't hard on me at all, it just fell in place, like anything I do, seemed regular, wasn't really a big deal." Soon after moving to Baltimore and starting classes in her new school, Serenity had already settled into a routine:

I have a boring 8 a.m. 50–min psychology class every Monday, Wednesday and Friday. It kills me to wake up to this class because it's so boring and this professor talks so slow! Tuesday and Thursday are my heavy days: I have four classes back to back at an hour and 20 minutes each, starting at 9:30 a.m., ending at 3:20 p.m., with just a 10–minute break in between each–just enough time to walk to my other classes. The classes are okay, I have World Lit II, Anthropology, Social Welfare Policy and Research Topics in Social Work. I'm a junior now so most of my classes are specifically around my major. I'm not working this semester so I feel very dull and bored–I need a job. All I do after class is go straight to my room, no play, just study!

Serenity regularly posted to Facebook from her mobile phone during her psychology class, complaining about how boring it was and how hard it was for her to stay awake. She also was not long without a job; within a few weeks of beginning the school year, she had added a part-time job to her list of tasks. During the summer breaks, she returns to New York City where she lives with her guardian and works multiple jobs, saving money for school. She sometimes complains about being too busy, yet she acknowledges that if she did not have all the schoolwork and jobs, she would not know what to do with her time; she likes to be very busy.

Genevieve was initially embarrassed about her struggles during her first semester away, especially because she had been so excited to leave home for college. When she "started over" at community college, she carried with her the residual anxiety of her struggles, and was nervous that she would repeat negative patterns. Because she had failed or dropped all her classes, she did not have any credits to transfer, so in her first semester in community college it was as if she had never been to college at all, yet she carried with her the lessons learned. Soon after starting classes, she spoke hesitantly about her plans:

> Technically I'm just starting out, this is my first semester. And I'm taking basic courses, my prerequisites, so it's nothing interesting. I mean, I know the basic elements of writing the essay already, so that's not really challenging me. I'm not taking a math course right now, but I will be taking it in the summer, so that probably will be challenging. I'm taking Art of Theater, English 101 and Environmental Ethics.

She soon realized that the community college environment was more supportive and suited to her needs than she initially thought:

> I'm fully engaged and the teachers, they work with you–not necessarily holding your hand, but they still work with you–so you still have that support system. And my classes are small, too, so that also helps a lot. When I was away, it was lecture halls and there was like 200 kids, and I didn't know anybody. And now, I have what is known as a cluster class where it's sort of like high school, I have the same kids and we go to different classes together, so I'm definitely connected with them, I know them, I'm able to call them if I'm missing homework, but it looks like they're calling me if they miss the homework. I just feel more con-

nected to the campus, it's a personal campus, which I really enjoy, and it does affect my academics in a positive way.

Within a year, Genevieve was a class leader and also had gotten the lead in the school play. She spoke more positively about her experience in October 2010:

> Classes are going well so far. I have a schedule where it is easy for me to balance schoolwork and rehearsals so that the two won't conflict. Things at home are still the same, Mom and Grandma are still nuts and I am still coping with being home and not away. I have tried to put what happened behind me but I feel like I relive it every time people asked me what happened, so it still stings a bit but I'm ok. I am just taking each day one step at a time.

Some participants do not feel that their lives have changed very much, especially those who attend local community colleges where they have not left the confines of their familiar space. Last, who wanted to take a year off but managed only a semester because of pressure from his mother, attends a community college in his neighborhood. He does not perceive much change, other than the absence of a peer community. "It's like going to class without the school. There are a lot of middle-aged people just trying to further their life that has already started. College is nothing like high school. The only similarities are homework and the requirement that you pay attention." However, sometimes it is the familiar geography and routine that cause struggles. Natalie attends a community college in her neighborhood, and initially she felt that little had changed. "It's okay, college. You don't really make friends that you keep in contact with. It's more of you go to class, do your homework and that's it. My high school I feel was more comfy than my college but I guess this just motivates you to do your work instead of hang out." However, about seven months later, Natalie experienced some significant personal and financial upheavals that made her academics suffer:

> Life is a bit hectic right now. Both my dogs were hospitalized in April and I now owe $3,000 in pet bills. I've been working as much as I can, therefore school has been suffering. The area I live in is becoming dangerous to my two younger brothers. They have been stopped and asked to empty out their pockets or get shot many times this year. I fear for their lives, and now we have a downstairs neighbor who sells drugs and gets into midnight fights and shakes the whole building, therefore I'm tired in the morning. I hate my life only because everything in it is in shit mode due to the lack of money. I still work in a supermarket. School is horrible, I'm currently filing for an academic appeal because my aunt died in Nicaragua last year so I was left as the stepparent.

Despite these struggles, Natalie has no plans to drop out of school and has asked my advice on how to choose a major that will facilitate her career plans in criminal justice. "School is horrible" because she cannot pay it the attention it needs and she longs for the familiar security of high school. Clearly her safety and the safety of her family need to be prioritized above school, but she knows completing school will make career options more plentiful in the long run. As she grapples with these problems, Natalie often posts short comments to Facebook such as "so stressed!!!" or "$$ problems suck!!!" with little to no further explanation. Based on our interviews and conversations, it seems that these posts are intended to release tension and seek support on the assumption that her Facebook friends know what is happening in her world.

Some participants experience burnout that, without a strong support system, could be detrimental. Eager her first year, Stacey suffered a bit during her sophomore year. After a tough semester she explained, "I think I lost the fire I had when I first applied to college. I either got too comfortable or I got intimidated by my surroundings at school. From the professors to some of the students I am around. You really realize the disadvantages you have compared to others." Despite all the things her father bought for her while they were briefly reunited, her two years in college reminded her that she had a greater economic struggle than her classmates, setting her at a marked disadvantage. Nevertheless, the participants in college feel that it is important to choose a field of study that matters to them.

Many of the participants speak decisively about their choice of major, even if they do not see a direct career path. Given their economic struggles, it might seem as if they are romanticizing their college experience, but it is important to articulate that despite economic upheavals, the participants want to follow their passions:

> *Genevieve:* I've always been interested in theater. Ever since I saw the movie version of *Annie*, I wanted to be on Broadway. As I began to get older, I started to doubt myself and become reserved. Since none of the schools I ever attended had theater programs, I was never able to fully explore that side of me. After my initial college fiasco, I decided to stop being so afraid of myself and do something for me, something that will make me happy. So that's why I decided to major in theater. I still don't know where it will take me, but I'm enjoying the ride while it lasts. Besides, my educational career won't stop at an A.S in theater, I also plan on getting my B.A in English.

Helena, Jacline and Jasmine have chosen majors that match careers they desire:

> *Helena:* I want to major in fashion photography because I really love the whole aspect of setting up for a shoot, finding the right model, clothes, makeup and so on. I also love how it's what YOU want it to be exactly and the whole editing process. Although the editing part is the longest part, it is all worth it at the end because I love the result. It's a little hard to find a studio to shoot in since it costs a lot of money, and I'm not always getting paid for the shoot in the first place. Sometimes the editing doesn't come out the way I want it at all and I get very frustrated, but I never let that stop me because I know that the industry is very

hard and it's only going to get harder. I want to do photography because it's an escape from things I don't like. I want to stay living in the city so I have to make it big in order to get paid big.

Jacline: My planned career path is to become an architect. I got interested in architecture because as a child I was exposed to architecture and engineering. Engineering was my father's career, and my aunt was in school to become an architect, so as time passed I developed an interest in the subject and it became a passion of mine. In high school I decided to turn my attention to it and now it is my planned career path. Architecture still amazes me now as much or even more than it did when I was a child and watched as my idols furthered themselves in the career. Architecture is an amazing subject, it is very complex and it never stops making me want to know more. The main things that make good architecture are having a structure that serves the specific function it was intended for and also has beauty and the visual characteristics that make it what it should be. Keeping in mind that "beauty" means different things to different people and that beauty changes over time. Architecture in this way leaves its mark in history. Knowing this, learning more about architecture, exploring the field by seeing my ideas come to life and my questions answered was what developed my interest in architecture.

Jasmine: I have found my passion for the hospitality industry during my two years in college. I will be studying abroad in Florence during next fall semester and participating in an international culinary program to gain hospitality experience overseas. I am majoring in hospitality management and doing a minor in marketing.

It is clear that Helena, Jacline and Jasmine have internalized the requirements of their planned careers: Helena will work hard to "make it big" in the city; Jacline knows the value of a functional, sound structure; and Jasmine recognizes the importance of traveling overseas to gain experience.

Some participants start off with one major and then when they learn more about it, change to something else. For Snapper in particular, this might mean that he needs to be in school longer, which he believes will be worthwhile in order to do what he loves:

I was always interested in structures, so when I was applying for college I knew I was going to have to look at engineering schools. I was still confused as to which major I wanted to get into, so since I also liked messing with electronics a lot, I thought I'd try electrical engineering. When I found out about civil engineering and its transportation branch I knew that was something I'd want to get into so I switched.

Now that he has switched to a vocational school in the city and has a job with the New York City Transit Authority, he is able to focus his attention to civil engineering. Over time, as they complete their coursework, the participants begin to see themselves as experts in their fields, speaking more concretely about their subject of choice. In May 2009, after his first year of college, Popcorn decided to be a literature major, for a variety of reasons:

> I see literature like this: Communication is important. And literature provides communication in the sense of like speaking and writing. You know what I mean, if you can write well, you're set. Like, you're good. I mean, look at everybody that was great in history. They all knew how to write well, they all knew how to speak well. Look at Benjamin Franklin, Frederick Douglass, like all these people, really brilliant writers. If you're a brilliant writer, I feel there's nothing you can't do. If you know how to communicate well and communicate with people directly, you're good. You can do anything. So that's why I chose to do it.

A year later, in May 2010, he refined his perspective on being a literature major:

> I feel like over the past year in school, I really understand literature more. I really understand what it's about. Essentially. Enough so much that I can really gauge if I want to do it or not, especially in this economy and this world. It is something that I want to do. And I'm really sure about it, I am now naturally going to critique and really look and take apart everything. Reading is something that's really easy for me now. I can really sit down with a book and read for mad hours. I don't know where that came from, like before it wasn't that easy. In high school, I didn't read that much. But now reading is something I *can* do and something I *like* to do. And I know I like to do it and I do it if it is for class or not even for class.

Popcorn admits to anxiety that literature is not a "practical" major, so he works towards internships that will develop his practical skills. He also debates whether to go directly after graduation to graduate school where he knows he can keep thinking but not necessarily make any money for an extended period of time. Making money, of course, remains a concern, and some participants forgo college entirely in order to start work immediately.

Work Life

A few participants have no plans to attend college. They realize this will impact their professional and career development, and they either do not care or do not feel that college is something at which they would excel. Johnny explains, "As of right now, working two jobs, trying to get a third." Johnny works at an ice skating rink in Queens and on a cruise ship that tours around New York City for private parties. He hopes that the third job he seeks will alleviate some financial pressures.

Lucy, who works as a security guard, explains her reason for not attending college:

College isn't for me. I thought about it, but while in college, I could lose out on a lot of money and experience in the work field. I feel that if I were to go to college it would be too hard to work and go to school. I just can't sit in a classroom for another two to four years listening to someone talk shit all day! And I'd be missing out on work and money.

Lucy expresses a concern common to young people who must work to pay their own bills: Two to four years in college does cost a lot of money, and in the meantime, it is difficult to make enough money to live comfortably, especially in New York City.

Nino tried college two times, once in New York City and once in California, but did not like sitting in class. Now she is trying to start her own business developing the skate crew brand she helped found in high school. Like Lucy, Nino explains, "School wasn't for me." She admits to feeling lost immediately after graduating from high school. While she attended community college she still worked at her old high school, which was a source of comfort and security, but she knew she was not moving forward. So she moved across the country to California, where she attended a state school. She loved California and the experience of being in a place totally different from New York City, but she did not love the school: "I didn't like the way I was being taught, but I stuck with it for a year to see if I would change my mind or get better but it didn't. So I chose to leave and find a better school that works for me." She now takes correspondence courses in photography; she is mailed a CD of lessons which she listens to on her own time, then she completes the work and mails it in.

Leaving NYC

One of the markers of adulthood is moving away from home and starting a life independent of one's parental/guardian family. For many of the participants who left home or left New York City, this experience proved too difficult. Some have chosen not to leave the city because, as Bruce explains, "New York City is my safe haven, it's my native town and I have a ton of support from family and more opportunities here than elsewhere." A few have left and returned, believing New York is the place where they need to be. Lucy was sent to California because she was getting into too much trouble in New York, and she thought about staying there but ultimately changed her mind:

I was going to move and stay. Maybe I could have gone places in the military, and some people might think it was a mistake by coming back to NYC, but I disagree. My love for Diamond isn't a mistake and I love where I'm at right now. I love to work (well, nobody really does) but I'm ok here. I love NY, there's no place like New York!

Nino also moved to California and loved the experience of living far away but did not like the college she was attending, so she moved back to New York for practical reasons. "I loved being there but I didn't enjoy the classes, which were three hours each every day. So I choose to move back and save my parents some money."

Both Genevieve and Jacline were excited for the traditional college dorm experience, but they had such difficult times adjusting that they felt much better when they returned:

> *Genevieve:* I briefly moved out of the city and into a college dorm. It was a different and exciting experience for me at first because I craved the freedom from my family and from the city (so I thought). I enjoyed the freedom that I had but I soon learned it became all too much for me. I was too young and too immature to handle what time to go to bed or when I should study. I know those seem like simple things to figure out but for me, it was a new concept because I was always under the watchful eye of my mother and her rules for me. To suddenly now be on my own was too much for me to handle at that time, and I feel like I went to this college away from home for all the wrong reasons. So I came back home to go to school and I'm happy that I did

> *Jacline:* After high school I moved out of the city and attended a state college. The experience was amazing and unique, but being on my own in a new place and taking on something so foreign to me as being a college student was difficult. I got sick and missed my family and found it hard to juggle everything on my own without the support of those close to me. So I decided to go back home and get used to college life here at home, before I do leave again, which I would definitely want to do in the future.

Although both young women ultimately want to move out of New York City for the experience of being away, for now they realize they need to learn a certain independence before that is possible.

Snapper enjoyed being away from New York City for a bit and liked the varied experiences of city and suburban life:

> My school is about four hours from here on the New York State Thruway. It's a nice experience, the school is like between a suburban and a rural area so I get to experience two different lifestyles at once. It's pretty relaxing actually. I'm away from all of the noise and everything up there is slow-paced.

Nevertheless, he is now back in New York City for the foreseeable future.

Jasmine, Peter, Serenity, Stacey and Popcorn all have a more traditional college experience that entails leaving home for semesters and returning to New York City between semesters, an experience they believe is valuable:

Jasmine: I moved upstate. Living there has exposed me to great opportunities in a suburban area that the city doesn't have to offer. Since attending college, I learned to dress warmer when conquering severe cold weather. I also learned to adapt to a new environment that involves driving, walking, or taking the bus to local restaurants and stores. I was able to meet diverse people from all over the world and discover insightful information about their culture.

Peter: I needed to get out of New York. It's too cluttered. If you stay here too long, you're bound to fail. We all need to get out and come back.

Serenity: I'm in B-more–the only thing I can say is their public transportation is the worst! New York runs 24 hours; here, there is a cut-off at around midnight.

Stacey: Long Island is not that different. I know the area pretty well because my grandmother lives here. I feel as if I gained more freedom. It's kind of like having a home away from home–when my mom gets on my nerves, I have a place to go and if my roommates get on my nerves, I have another place to go.

Popcorn: It's really different from the city, 'cause it's like: The woods! You're like, in the woods! It's really ill 'cause you have animals, like deer and raccoons and all that ill stuff–I prefer the deer and raccoons to rats and cockroaches because they're outside and nice to look at. It's like really just beautiful, like in the spring, it's lovely. I sort of didn't want to leave–I wanted to leave, 'cause it's school–but that area's wonderful to be in. It's like really quiet and like a lot of birds and it's really like naturey. Being out of the city, you can look at it objectively. And really sort of understand it, being away from it.

What leaving New York City has done for these participants, even when they leave only for semesters, is show them how other parts of the world work. Both Jasmine and Popcorn saw how the world works in foreign countries, but they also talk about their experiences with the unfamiliarity of their college campuses. What is revealed is that even travelling as close to home as upstate New York, Baltimore, or down South is a profound experience. These experiences are different for each individual, and Chapter Six focuses on Genevieve and Popcorn, exploring their transition more thoroughly.

SIX

"All That Freedom...":
Two Stories of College Success

When Genevieve, a young African American woman, graduated from high
school in 2009, she was eager to leave New York City and escape the restrictions set by her overprotective mother and grandmother. She moved six hours
north to attend a private university. In December Genevieve was back in New
York City and back at her mother's apartment: She had failed out of the university. She realized she was unhappy living so far from home, attending large lecture
classes where she did not know her professors, and among mostly white students.
What she thought she wanted—freedom—ended up being what strangled her. After
three months back in New York City, Genevieve enrolled in a local community
college where she excelled in her classes, landed the lead role in the school play,
and became the one her classmates asked for studying help, and she began to
forge an adult, mutually respectful relationship with her mother. Reflecting on
her months of serious depression, which she believes started during her senior
year in high school when she first planned to move away from home, Genevieve
sighs, shakes her head and exclaims, "All that freedom.... " She implies that too
much freedom, without structure or boundaries, can be overwhelming.

Popcorn, who graduated the year before Genevieve, had a very different experience. Popcorn chose a state university about an hour from New York City,
and when he realized during his freshman year that he was not fully prepared for
university-level work, spent extra hours in the library studying and preparing for

courses. By the start of his senior year he had a routine down and felt fully prepared for the expectations of his last year of college.

These two participants tell very different stories. In their years out of high school and into college they have chosen their own paths, acknowledged their struggles and worked to create spaces where they feel successful. Success has no single definition and their stories illustrate the multiple avenues that can be taken to achieve success. Both maintain their social connections with the important supportive people in their lives and use Facebook to share stories and keep updated when far away from these people. Both also follow an approach to school that is less career oriented and more focused on the experience of learning. This chapter spends concentrated time with both Genevieve and Popcorn to illustrate their great efforts and the lessons they learned along the way that teach them about the power structures and systems that organize their environments.

Genevieve

Genevieve transferred to LSHS at the start of her sophomore year and was immediately recognized as an outstanding student. She soon developed a cohort of friends in her grade and a fair number of friends in the grade ahead of her because she was placed in junior-level math and science classes. Genevieve lived in Harlem with her protective mother, grandmother and brother, a young man with a severe mental disability. She was always a solid student, though sometimes she made careless errors that drove her to distraction and depression. She was afraid that her mistakes would make her teachers and family think less of her.

After her junior year in high school, Genevieve attended a summer program at an elite boarding school in Vermont. She was initially afraid that she would not fit in, that she would fail the required athletic component because of her size and that people would not like her because she was a dark-skinned African American from New York City. In fact, she had an amazing experience and the taste of being away from home and away from the city solidified her desire to go away to college. Her mother was nervous about letting Genevieve even apply to college; she had tried college herself and as a single mother raising two children (including a son who needs constant care), while working and caring for her elderly mother, she feared that college could not fit into the mix. Genevieve fought her mother on this during her senior year, gaining ammunition when several private schools outside of New York City accepted her and offered her partial scholarships. Much to her mother's dismay, Genevieve was determined not only to go to college but also to get out of New York City.

I spoke with Genevieve shortly after the holidays following her first semester away. When we got on the phone, she began defensively, "So, what have you heard?" I had not heard anything at that point. Her friends tended to have more tumultuous lives, so at first I assumed there was some gossip about them. It took some convincing to assure her that I knew nothing, but by that point, she seemed hesitant to tell me; it was as if she was hoping I had heard about her experiences from someone else and she would not need to explain the whole story. Finally she sighed, "You know, it didn't really work out so well. Being that my grades weren't that great." Through a series of conversations I learned that it was not just that her grades were not "that great": She had failed or dropped out of all of her classes and was back in New York City in a serious depression.

The problems started in the fall, as discussed in Chapter Three, when she started to feel overwhelmed by the workload. She struggled in a Biology of Sex class, failing the first test, and was not able to recover from that:

> I think I passed one test and then another. I needed a high score and then there was another test that I failed. I spoke with the professor and he was like, "In order to pass this class, you have to do exceptionally well in this and this," and I was like oh crap. Ultimately, he said there was no way I could pass the class, even if I took the final, so he was like, "If you have any other classes that you need to focus your time on, you should do that, and I wish you the best." So basically I had to drop that class. And then there were the other classes. I felt I was doing well, except for one where I was putting things off 'til the last minute. And one day I just didn't catch up. It was a snowball effect: The readings accumulated, I wasn't able to pass with high marks on some of the quizzes and exams, and that accumulated, too. So I talked to *that* professor, to see if I was able to do her essays over or do this extra credit that I was working on and I could pass the class. I'm like okay, and I'll do it, fine, get that out the way so that when other classes–this is finals time, now–so there's other classes that need essays from me, too. And on top of those essays, I need to do finals. So I was freaking out, it was the week before finals and I had all these papers to do. And I just cracked. I lost sleep, I didn't eat, I was up like at 5 o'clock in the morning and since that 9 o'clock class was out, you know, I was able to have an extra hour before then, but then I also scheduled study sessions with my Italian teacher for work, to improve in her class, I was doing okay, but still, since I officially had an F in one class, I needed to bring her class up so that F wouldn't affect me.

Genevieve became so overwhelmed that she stopped sleeping, stopped eating, could not focus and eventually did not leave her room. She reached out to a close cousin who encouraged her to tell her mother, but she was too scared:

> Like I said before, I cracked. And once I realized that I wasn't gonna pass that se-mester, I just literally broke down on the phone with my cousin. And you know, he was telling me, "You gotta tell your mom, you gotta tell your mom. You have to go home." 'Cause at that point, I was thinking, I can't go home, I can*not* go home. I'm running away, I don't care if I go into prostitution, I can't go home. He was laughing at me, "Where you gonna go? Where you gonna live?" So, you know, I told my mom. And she took it well, you know, but I really, I felt like I didn't explain to her enough of the situation because she still felt like I had a

chance to pass. She just kept on telling me, "You can't give up, you gotta keep going." And that was hard because I knew that no matter what I did, I still wasn't going to be able to hand in everything, do everything and pass.

Genevieve did not intend to mislead her mother, but she was so surprised by her mother's support that she let her believe it was just a matter of getting through the end of the semester. It was not until she was back in New York during winter break, when she got a letter from the university explaining her academic suspension, that her mother found out the whole story. She and her mother prepared an appeal of the suspension, but having no experience with this procedure, they were not sure how to handle it. "My mom and I wrote the letter to appeal it. I did everything that they asked me to; they went over my grades again. Despite my two-page outline of how I was going to improve, they rejected me." She could have appealed the decision—"I could've gone back if I were to complete six credits of college courses, and then complete some other stuff, and then they would let me back in"—but as much as she did not like failing out, she did not want to return. She and her mother drove north to pack up Genevieve's belongings and officially withdraw her from school.

    Much to her surprise, her mother supported her interest in returning to college and the two worked together on applications to local city schools. However, because of the late date, Genevieve was too far behind to start any classes in the January term. So she looked into applying to schools as a freshman in the fall, hoping she could put the whole first semester behind her, but she was not sure how she would explain the lost year. She returned once again to the familiar staff of LSHS for help: "I was looking to apply for fall semester as a freshman, and I had all these questions and concerns and I didn't know how to do that without them knowing that I already was in college. I had no other choice but to go back to the school." When she confided in the assistant principal, guidance counselor and college advisor, these three women told Genevieve's teachers what had happened. Though she feels they were trying to be helpful and trying to gather information on her behalf, Genevieve was mortified when she had to reach out for help:

> I didn't think my mom had much experience dealing with college and stuff like that, college admissions, so I had to suck up my pride and go back to high school. And talk to my college advisor. And that was my biggest fear, just facing everybody, their judgments of me, their assumptions. Little did I know, my news of me being back in town and the reasons why were known by all of my teachers. So my fears came true and I just felt all the shame that I held inside, just come streaming out.

She retreated home and grew increasingly depressed. She soon learned that a local community college had trimesters, and instead of waiting for the fall, she could start classes in March, which was just a few weeks away. The time off had made her realize how much she wanted to be in school, how unprepared she had been the first time around, her own culpability in what had happened and how outside forces had contributed to her difficulties:

> I realized I had a couple of problems with completing work. I realized that after awhile, it just caught up to me. Time management skills and procrastination, all that stuff. So that just finally caught up with me. And that kind of led to my downfall. You know, this happened for a reason, I'm trying to reflect and sort of change, I don't know how, though, but I just have this time to figure it out. I really don't want to be out of school. I really don't want to be out of school, that's torture, but I wouldn't go back there. I mean, even if my grades were okay, and I mean I had everything else figured out, I still wasn't really happy up there.

Genevieve had thought about transferring soon after she moved north. She realized quickly that she was not suited to the environment but she did not want things to end as they did:

> I wish things could have ended differently, you know, I finish up the year and then transfer. I don't like the way it ended. But I just have to move on, that's what I'm trying to tell myself. And it's keeping me from crying at night. And I'm just looking at this as a fresh start and I think that this will make me a lot stronger.

While Genevieve places most of the blame on herself, she is aware that there were other factors that were difficult for her to handle. She was very involved in campus life and rediscovered some of her theatrical and musical interests, but she could not seem to make herself at home at school:

> The weather didn't do it for me, either. I didn't see the sun for two months. I felt like I was getting around to making friends and everything. And I had quite a few. But I just felt out of place there. I mean, everybody else loved it there, they called it their home, you know, they felt like themselves and I felt like this wasn't where I was supposed to end up. Something's not right. I had a job, I was involved in groups. I got back into singing again, which I always wanted to do. If that didn't make me happy, I don't know what would. I just wasn't happy. So, I was gonna transfer anyway, but I didn't like the way things ended up, but you know what, I can't really change what happened, and I'm going forward from here.

She was initially disappointed that her only immediate option was to attend community college. She felt that was yet another failure on her part, to go from a private university with scholarship money to a community college, and she worked to stay positive about the experience. She was mostly grateful that she did not have to just sit around for several more months, waiting for the fall semester.

After much deliberation, she also finally admitted that the lack of ethnic diversity in upstate New York was difficult for her. As a dark-skinned, heavy-set African American woman, she did not feel that she fit in with the rest of the student body, despite making a healthy collection of friends:

> Okay, I'ma be honest, that school was real white. It was real white. I couldn't stand that part. I mean, at first, I'm like ok, I come from New York City, I should be more open-minded, but then, just looking at it from a real perspective, most of the time, I did feel isolated. And there were a lot of people that would not talk to me. I mean, there was a class where I had to interact with people and no one would want to talk to me. I felt so hurt. And I would see other people and they were happy and they were interacting with other people. And I couldn't get to that level. And I know it was first semester and I know people said it takes time or whatever.

She realized quickly she wanted a school with more ethnic diversity where she would see students who looked more like her and maybe a school that was in a more urban environment. She had been accepted to a school like this but did not receive enough financial aid to make the choice viable. She realizes that visiting schools before enrolling would have been valuable. "If I had visited upstate before I said yes, I would not have gone." She did not receive a full scholarship, so she and her mom took out loans that they must pay back without having earned a degree or any credits. Resigned to the situation, Genevieve prepared for community college to get an associate's degree so that maybe she can go away again. However, she and her mother are in a more precarious financial position because of the student loans, so going away is also "a financial aid thing. Because my mom helped me with my loans. So I not only screwed myself, I screwed her over, too. She said I keep on messing up stuff." Genevieve knew she could not afford the school when she accepted the offer of a place:

> My mom, she sucked it up and she tried, she did whatever she could in order for me to get into that school. And then, screwing up the first semester. She doesn't fully, you know, convey her anger, but you know, it slips out once in a while. And I know I hurt her. I can't put her through that again. Yeah, that's all I want to do, I mean, she really expected me to crash again. You know, she's asking me, "Why aren't you upset?" like I'm supposed to cry every day or be angry at the world every day.

Genevieve looks at her peers who chose not to attend college and sees their struggles and knows she wants to be in school:

> I look at some kids from my graduating class, they didn't go to college right away, or they're not going at all, or they had kids or whatever, and all this other stuff. And they're miserable. That is just not my life. I see myself going to school

and I don't know what I want to do with my life, I don't know what kind of career I want to go into, but there's a lot of stuff I'm interested in and I just can't get that out of a 9 to 5 job. That doesn't sit with me.

During the first trimester at the local community college, Genevieve's spirits had improved, she was feeling productive on a daily basis and had become a class leader. She was able to look back at her breakdown and see how far she had come:

After I moved back, well, it was a rough time. I had to adjust being back home and being my mother's child again. That was tough coming from an environment where I can frolic in the snow at 2 a.m. and you know, still go to class at 7 a.m. And then I have to cut back a little bit because, again, I am my mother's child and I have to get back in that role. I am in my mom's house again and I have to follow her rules. So that adjustment was a little bit difficult. And also, the adjustment of not being in school. 'Cause I mean, I left after one semester. So, in my family and my community, I just had to face so many questions and so many assumptions that they had, "Oh you're on break?" And it's sort of hard to say, "No, I'm actually back home for good." Most of them were rooting for me, they just really enjoyed seeing one of their own away in college, out of New York City, getting an education. I felt like I was disappointing a lot of people and that just made my getting back on my feet, my adjustment back home, a little bit harder.

However, starting at another college renewed Genevieve's resolve, and she felt like a productive member of society again:

At first, it just felt good to be back in school again, to say to people on the street, "I can't talk right now, I'm going to school." And not just hold my head down anymore. I'm actually doing something with my life. And I just felt so proud of myself that I was getting back on my feet and not letting what happened to me defeat me. So my first experience of the school, I just love it. I love all my classes. I'm a theater and communications major. And I didn't think, first of all, I would declare a major so soon, that I would actually make up my mind. For the first time actually in my life, I have a plan and I'm actually doing something that I enjoy, that you know, no one has forced me into doing. And I'm just loving my life right now. I'm back in school, my relationship with my mom is better. I thought it was going to be worse. Now that I had to go back into, you know, daughter role. Supporter role. You know, for the family and stuff like that. She's giving me more freedom 'cause she realizes that I'm no longer a kid anymore. And that I'm a woman. I'm really enjoying that. I just feel like I'm moving again. And before, when I came home, I felt like I was just stuck. And all my friends that were in college or doing their job or having their family or whatever, they were just moving along with their life. And I felt like I was just being left behind. Now I have my own life and I'm moving on. So, I'm really happy right now.

A year later, Genevieve remains happy and committed to her community college program. With greater distance, she is able to reflect on high school and see that the poor choices she made in college were due in large part to a lack of preparation for the independent learning and self-motivation needed in college. She feels that her high school "taught down" to her and her classmates because they were un-derserved, impoverished youth. She feels that attending a start-up school meant that there were too many experiments done in the name of creative, alternative education which, while engaging at the time, did not adequately prepare them for college life:

> It was a start-up school, unfortunately, they were still finding their way and we were in the midst of that. I don't think you should be experimenting with chil-dren's education. It's too delicate of a subject to be experimenting with. Either there should be a different approach to it, or you gotta find something else 'cause this way did not work. I mean, now we're just struggling to find our way out of all the mess, all the chaos and just trying to develop those studying habits, and to pass those classes that we now have to face. That we weren't exactly prepared for.

Genevieve acknowledges that some of her classmates adjusted well, that there are indeed people who can handle the transition without undue struggle, but she does not count herself among them:

> There are some people out there who are able to handle that adjustment and some people aren't. I'm an example of that. I'm a prime example. I failed my first semester. And I'm not blaming the school entirely, 'cause, I am my own person, I have free will. But I mean, if I really was academically prepared and confident, then I probably would have finished that semester positively and then been able to make that decision, okay, I'ma transfer schools now, I did what I could here and I can move on.

Genevieve did not fail out because she was engaging in risky, unhealthy behavior but because she was overwhelmed. Part of the reason she was overwhelmed was that she lacked a support system or knowledge of places to reach out to when in crisis. Certainly, part of the reason she was in this state was because her high school did not prepare urban youth from impoverished backgrounds to handle the day-to-day life of a private college where most students come from back-grounds of much greater social and economic privilege. In addition, while her professors took the time to help her, she was not aware if the college had formal supports for students who have the intellectual promise that warranted admission but also life experiences that make it unusually difficult to overcome challenges. At this point, Genevieve is able to see only what she and her high school did wrong; the bigger picture is how the strictures of the system make it challenging to break certain barriers. Do support systems that reach out to students of color at predominantly white universities serve as a further reminder of how different someone like Genevieve is from the mainstream?

Acknowledging her own struggles and the strength she gained from a strong support system at home, Genevieve argues for the importance of support for individuals. Although she still believes that her mother was way too overprotective, she is now aware that her mother is deeply invested in her future, unlike the parents of some of her close friends. She believes that people deserve much greater systemic support to get them through times of struggle:

> I never fit in as a child. I was always too much of this or too much of that. With the exception of some really good friends, I couldn't connect with most people. If I didn't have such a great support system, I probably wouldn't have cared so much about my life. Some kids go through their life without making any profound connections with other people. They almost feel invisible. I would know, I felt that way a lot during junior high, some parts of high school and my first semester of college. I think the most important thing to do is to hold on to something stable in your life, whether it be writing in a journal, your religion, a hobby, anything that gets you out of that dark place. If you make yourself believe that there is nothing left, there won't be, unless you look.

Genevieve now has a life plan; undoubtedly this will change, but what she feels is important is that she has clear goals, a greater perspective on struggle, and a more precise focus:

> I just want to get back on track again. I was explaining to one of my friends that this experience really taught me to go at my own pace. And not to let society's expectations dictate what you want to do in life. So, for the first time, this is my plan. I just wanted to get back on track with that, to just graduate from this two-year college, get my associate's degree in theater and communications, and to go to a four-year college and get a bachelor's in English, with a minor in media studies. And, if everything goes well and I get that far and I feel like I am ready to take that next step, I will get my master's, I think, continuing in English. I really love to write and I love the theater and I love media studies. There's just so many interests I have, so, taking my educational process step by step, from associate's to master's and that stuff just gives me, you know, a broad range in skills and experience. It's just part of me taking my time, you know, going at my own pace.

The importance of going at her own pace is what Genevieve ultimately feels she learned from her initial college experience. Originally, she told me the most important life lesson she had learned was "control." A year later, she revised that lesson, giving up her need for control and instead setting her own pace:

> Just go at your own pace. Just set a goal for yourself, don't listen—well, if anybody's giving you helpful advice, you know, of course, consider it—but don't be so overwhelmed just to do what everyone is telling you to do. You know, go to that private college and just graduate. I don't know the plan, just make a plan for yourself, go at your own pace, listen to yourself, do what works for you, what

you need to work on, don't be afraid to take risks, to challenge yourself, just listen to yourself and I guarantee, you'll just be happier.

Genevieve's story shows the reality for underserved youth who lack the invisible support of multiple generations of college attendance. As a student whose school "experimented" on her, she had little preparation for college life. Genevieve did not achieve success right away. Given the time, space and support from family and friends, she was able to make the transition to college. The change in her language over the course of her transition is important: She begins defensively ("So what have you heard?") and ends up more open-minded and philosophical ("Don't be afraid to take risks, to challenge yourself, just listen to yourself and I guarantee, you'll just be happier").

In contrast, Popcorn succeeded at college almost immediately, though he, too, was challenged by certain difficulties, and he had to give himself the space to work through them.

Popcorn

Popcorn was a member of the first graduating class of LSHS. He was a bright student, a gifted artist and dancer, and one of the most popular and friendly students in the school. Teachers, staff and students alike admired him. It was clear that Popcorn had a great deal of promise.

Upon graduation, he chose to attend a public college about an hour north of the city. He was both nervous about leaving his close friends, his mother and his sister, and excited by the prospect of going away to college, living in a dorm, and being involved in a well-established school. In the fall of his freshman year I visited Popcorn and while he was embarrassed for me to see his dorm room (he insisted his roommates were slobs), he was proud to show me the building where he lived, and he introduced me to various friends who were coming and going from class. Popcorn fit in right away, which, given his shyness, surprised him: He seemed amazed that people wanted to be friends with him because he is so quiet.

For the most part, Popcorn's transition to college is a success story, though it involved a lot of hard work, soul searching and reflection. At the end of his first year, after moving home for the summer, Popcorn remembered what it felt like when he first got to college:

When I left home, that was huge for me. Like the first night in my dorm, I was like, okay, this is entirely new, this is where it all begins. Because when I was in high school, I would lay in my room and I would like think about ways to get out of my room. My room as a metaphor for my current situation. I mean, how can I break out of these four walls? You know, what can I do on my end to make that happen for myself. And when I got there, I was like, okay, I did that. And

I'm proud of myself. But, now, now I'm coming into this new environment. A new room, metaphorically, what can I do to get used to it? To take advantage of it. And then eventually, break out of those four walls and get into something else.

Thinking metaphorically and philosophically about the four walls of his surroundings did not stop Popcorn from also thinking practically. He realized soon after getting to college that high school had not taught him how to balance freedom:

> Now I feel I'm in the second stage where I'm more allowed to do what I want to do and develop as a young adult. High school doesn't really provide that, it just basically keeps you boxed in. At least in my experience, it just kept me boxed in to the point where I was pent up with mad anticipation! When I was finding that I could release, like that's what I did, I just did stuff that I always wanted to do, that I wasn't allowed to do. Or learn things, you know what I mean? Just learn like really cool stuff that I wanted to learn, but I didn't know about.

Popcorn's first year in college was in many ways traditional: He left home, then became aware of how much he had left to learn—and how much he wanted to learn it—while also dealing with an alien social environment. He went from living with his mother in an apartment in Harlem to living with two other first-year students in a dorm room on campus. He went from seeing his very best friends every day to seeing them occasionally on weekends when they came up for parties or over holidays. He went from a social and school environment made up of bodies that looked mostly like him to a school environment that, while diverse, was more white than he had ever experienced. He grappled with the concept of friendship and how he wanted to maintain his long-term friends while also making new ones. In a conversation after their first year apart, he explains his struggle to Bruce and Peter:

> That was definitely like an issue for me, when I would like call you guys, me being like all the way upstate, you guys being in the city together and you guys would, you know, be like hanging out or at the movies, and like just chillin' at your crib, I would definitely be sad, you know, just sitting in my dorm, or at the library. Like at the library on a Friday night, it was definitely like an issue at first.

He remained reliant on Bruce and Peter for friendship, not venturing socially too far on his own. "It came to the point where I wouldn't go to parties on campus unless they were there. So if they weren't there, you wouldn't see me out. Eventually, I was like, I have to come into my own 'cause I'm here in this environment, so eventually, I got used to it." What Popcorn was not aware of was that Bruce and Peter envied him being out of the city, having a traditional college experience. They visited him to get a taste of that experience as much as to be with him.

In order to excel at college, Popcorn had to work harder than he ever had in high school. In high school studying was not an issue, and if work was not completed on time, all teachers would allow extra time. This was not the case in college; Popcorn spent much of his time freshman year in the library trying to develop better studying habits. This work paid off–he did very well in his first year–and he realized in sophomore year that knowing the routine did not mean he could relax:

> Sophomore year was emotionally very hard 'cause I had a girlfriend and school and like, some like minor family problems. It was sort of difficult navigating that and getting my priorities sort of like straight again. I felt like my priorities got mixed up, like, in a very bad way. And so I started hanging out more, and started doing more college stuff, like experimenting with drugs and all that. That just made it more difficult to get back to what I needed to do, and I would always like beat myself up about that because I knew what I had to do, I just wouldn't do it. Not to say that my grades were affected, I did fine, fall semester I got Bs across the board, so it wasn't that bad, compared to other kids or compared to what it could have been. But fall semester was really difficult.

Popcorn and I shared many conversations about the root of the word "sophomore" and how he felt like a "wise fool" who knew what to do but still made less productive choices. He struggled with time management, something that had been relatively easy when he was not attempting to be social at school and more difficult when he was trying to make friends and maintain a relationship with his girlfriend. For his grades to slip to Bs is not, in the big picture, a big deal. But for Popcorn, that and the negative way he felt after experimenting with drugs were enough to get him refocused. In the spring semester "I got things back in order and now I'm a little bit more confident in who I am and what I'm doing and decisions that I'm making and will be making." Overall, sophomore year was a time of personal growth:

> Sophomore year in college was feeling weird about myself. I'm sure that's what happens. You know, thinking that you know more, or that you're really smart, but you're really not. And sort of being full of yourself but then like knowing that and not being full of yourself and not being like confident at all. So it's just like weird contradictions.

He admits that some of the drug experimentation was fun and he learned a lot from it, but mostly he felt bad about it and insists, "Now I'm done with that, it was just whack."

What he learned in sophomore year was how to relax and be focused, but so many things happened at once during the year that he could not catch up. Between his girlfriend, classes and the immense social opportunities, he was caught up in the whirlwind. While Popcorn was tremendously social in high school, his environment there was much smaller: He regularly hung out and traveled the streets of New York City, but despite the breadth of offerings in the city, the crowd he ran with was small. At college, however, the scene changed:

The social scene isn't like what it's supposed to be, 'cause I went to a small high school, so everybody basically knew each other, everybody at least said hi to each other and was friendly with each other. But in college, it's not like that, even though it's small enough for it to be like that. It was like not having a group of friends like I had in high school, like that close, I don't have that at college. It's more difficult to access people for some reason. That in itself was difficult, so the drugs were just a way to act at ease, because like everybody on the weekends would get like really drunk, really high, and then talk to each other and have a great time. But then on Monday, nobody's really that friendly with each other 'cause we were all on drugs. So it's not natural. That was one of the major reasons why I was doing this stuff. But now that I have a good group of friends, now that I have these like significant relationships with people, I don't really need to be doing drugs anymore. I'm more secure, I know what this school has to offer and I know what it doesn't.

Though his college is small by state-school standards, it is much larger than his high school, and the excitement of meeting new people was depleted by sophomore year.

Popcorn was raised by a single mother. He has brothers and a sister and a cordial relationship with his father, but it is his mother he credits with teaching responsibility to make the right choices and to own up to his decisions:

'Cause she was always hard working and she always kept what she had to do top priority, regardless. It's mainly just looking at her and seeing how she operates and navigates the city and life. And it's kind of amazing. Not even "kind of," it really is. Our relationship now is way more mature, she doesn't really treat me as a child anymore. We have really significant conversations and we're really comfortable with each other. My mom, she knows I smoke weed, she doesn't like it, but she knows that I'm comfortable enough with her to tell her this. 'Cause she really trusts me and my decisions and how I go about things. And if I need help, she knows like I'll come to her, so our relationship really matured since I went to college. Our conversations go beyond simply "How are you? How's school?" "School's good." "Great." "Can you like give me money?" It's way beyond that.

He believes it was the support from his mother that helped him regain his focus: He did not want to disappoint her, and he saw her as a guiding force in his life.

Popcorn has a vulnerability and an eagerness to learn that contradicts stereotypes and assumptions of urban black men. He is aware of what he is "supposed" to be and how that differs from who he is:

Hard, tough, smart but street smart, not really into academia that much. Just focused on getting girls, that's what it is. Girls and money. And doing drugs. And lookin' fresh all the time and buying really expensive clothes. For no reason. And going to parties and shit. This is what I know from looking at acquaintances and friends. Living in the city and not really going to school, not really focused on school. Focused on technology, the newest phone, gotta get that. And I'm not really focused on that.

What Popcorn grappled with in May 2010 as he finished his sophomore year was how to make sense of what he had been exposed to thus far at college. He feels his studies have changed him, made him less street smart and more school smart. He feels a bit bad about this, as if he has betrayed his background, but knows that it is deeply important for his future:

> The things I talk about with people, I feel bad for wanting to talk about books or certain topics. To talk about the state of society in the 1920s, you know what I mean, and people aren't down to talk about that. I feel like maybe I'm being pretentious. But it's just things that I'm really interested in. And I been talking about these things over the course of three, four months so, you know, you get used to talking about that kind of stuff. And I'm not really into celebrities or pop culture so I can't talk about what Lady Gaga or L'il Wayne is doing, you know what I mean, so where do I stand in this world of change, you know what I mean? I don't know.

He laughs at his use of the word "pretentious," knowing that he would not have spoken like that if it were not for college. He further specifies that he would not have spoken like that if it were not for being a literature major, which he credits with teaching him to think critically:

> I feel it is because of my major and because literature is basically reading a lot and critiquing it and really like trying to understand it and interpreting it in different ways. That's translated into how I see everything. I'm always critiquing everything and I'm always looking at different ways to interpret people and their actions—I'm not supposed to do that! People aren't literature. Literature is literature and people are people. Even though literature like sort of represents people. So I'm trying to really understand that, to put it into practice. I don't want to seem like a know-it-all or like some dude that just wants to talk about Hemingway, or some shit like that. Nobody wants that guy around. *I* don't want that guy around!

Popcorn took a risk his junior year and applied to study abroad in Paris, even though he did not speak French. Overall, it was an extraordinary experience. He posted pictures and videos regularly on Facebook of his travels to Amsterdam, Brussels and around France. He found an abandoned bicycle on the streets of Paris and adopted it as his own; he was sad when he had to leave it behind, thinking it would be a great thing to have in New York. He trolled Parisian flea markets and bought old, broken cameras for just a few euros to see what he could do with them. After just three months, Paris felt like home and he had gained the travel-ler's appreciation for his true home, New York:

> Been here for three months now and it's really starting to feel like a second home. I walk through the neighborhood where I live saying "hi" to some of the people whom I've gotten to know here. It's a very relaxed lifestyle from my point of view as an international student. People here are as friendly as people in New York and also it seems that a lot of students here in my generation want to come to New York to live and work. I have a new appreciation for NYC now, being away from it for so long, and I see America as something different from before. This I can't really find words for. New York for me now is the most important city in our world and therefore while it is a part of America it is not an American city. It's a world city. Just seeing the differences has been very interesting to me.

Classes in Paris proved to be tough because he did not speak the language:

> School here has been tough. As you know I did not speak French before coming to France and all classes are taught in French. My advisor and the dean of my program thought it would not be such a good idea doing a program like this considering my language level, but the program director stated it would be fine considering that it's a language immersion. I see now that both sides were right. I can currently understand French. Not fluently but enough to get by on a day-to-day basis considering that I did not know a single word three months ago. It is still difficult to follow everything the professor says as two of my classes are huge lectures with maybe 80–100 kids.

After his sophomore year trials, Popcorn brought his grades back up and was con-cerned that Paris might have a negative impact on his GPA:

> I am extremely terrified how my GPA could be affected by this because I can definitely say I won't be getting As in these courses. I'm technically a senior un-dergrad this coming fall and will have to complete a senior project in the field of literature. As far as a specific topic I have no fucking clue but I have all summer to think about it.

Although he claims to have no clue what to do, the evidence that Popcorn's learn-ing has had an impact on his thinking is clear when he ruminates about a possible topic:

> I do know however that I'm interested in language systems in the 21st cen-tury over the past 10 years and the development of new words, new feelings, anxieties, questions and media through which these new phenomena are com-municated since 9/11, since for me (and I'm sure for the rest of the world), the 21st century began on that day. However, I feel like it's not clear enough and I don't really know if the literature faculty would even accept such a proposal. Plus how can I even link that to traditional literature? I don't know. We'll see. I know that the intended purpose of a senior project is to show that we as students

have inherited the tradition of our study so that we may take it further and add to the field. Most students do critiques on their favorite writers and poets, like Dostoyevsky and Walt Whitman, which is freaking awesome 'cause those guys are awesome, but I don't want to do that. I know this is just a senior project; a simple 60–page paper, and it won't change the world but I just want to make it interesting for me so I actually enjoy doing it.

Both Popcorn and Genevieve have travelled so far in a few short years. Like Genevieve's, Popcorn's language changes. In 2009 he spoke about the importance of literature as a tool of communication, as discussed in Chapter Five. In 2011 he inquires how words, feelings, anxieties, questions and media have shifted since 9/11, the symbolic start to the 21st century. Both Popcorn and Genevieve experienced an environment very different from home and had very different responses. While Popcorn's school is more ethnically diverse than Genevieve's, it too is predominantly white. Broadly speaking, the university system as a whole follows a traditionally white, middle- to upper-class route to success, despite increased matriculation by students of color. In the face of neoliberalism, the university rewards individual achievement over a community connection of interdependence. Why was Popcorn able to adapt to that different environment more easily than Genevieve? Because he is male? Because of his closer proximity to New York City? There is no clear answer to this question and what is more important is that both Genevieve and Popcorn took time to explore their intellectual and social needs, for time is a precious commodity that not all young people can afford. Are Popcorn and Genevieve just lucky, or do they possess superior navigation skills?

Both Genevieve and Popcorn come from backgrounds where finding support for their intellectual growth is a continuous challenge. The system is set up to fail them. Yet they have managed to navigate the system to their satisfaction. As they prepare to move out of college and into the next stage of their lives, will they continue to succeed? Will they be models for the next generation of urban youth? Chapter Seven revisits several of the participants, sharing their words of advice as a guiding frame to conclude this text. What changes need to be made to the larger system of education in order to develop more success stories? Education is notoriously slow to change, despite all the political rhetoric about the need for aggressive reform, yet technology changes extremely rapidly. Can lessons learned from social networking be used to improve education? Chapter Seven addresses these concerns to offer a plan of what can be done to make beneficial change for all students.

SEVEN

Conclusion:
What Now?

Chapter Six focused on the stories of Genevieve and Popcorn as they maneuvered their way through the transition from high school to college and through their successes and trials. There is no one answer why these two individuals succeeded where others have failed. Correspondingly, there is no one answer why others such as Johnny and Lucy believe that college is more effort than it is worth. Successes and trials must be explored and interrogated: Is Genevieve successful because she moved home? Because the workload at community college is less demanding than at a private university? Because the experience of failure jump-started her motivation? Because in New York City there are more familiar faces and more bodies that look like Genevieve? Is the fear of intellectual failure enough to keep Johnny out of the classroom? Is the very real need to make money in the short term enough pressure to keep Lucy away from school (though it might ultimately prevent her from earning more money in the long term)? The participants' stories show that the rhetoric of school reform does not produce real, positive changes in their high school tenure and their movement from high school to college or work. Much work remains to better understand the present state of education reform and the ways in which reforms are ineffective in improving the situations of many young people.

Let us listen more closely to the participants as they offer advice to the next generation of students about making the transition from high school into college and work. I use their words to make sense of the environment in which they find themselves and to argue for an intervention of critical media literacy to help make positive change in the public school system. Their advice is not just for the next generation of high school graduates, but also, more importantly, for those concerned with education and the future of public schooling.

Media literacy can provide the means for a vital intervention. Train young people to think analytically and to learn the unfamiliar through the process of critical inquiry—the foundation of critical media literacy—and they will strengthen their schools and, in turn, strengthen their communities. Not all young people must be activists but they deserve to be critically *aware* participants in their own civic growth. Critical media literacy is a tool for approaching new topics of study, for examining the ubiquitous presence of the mainstream media in our society and for drawing on the digital mobile media with which young people are already so familiar. It can be used to connect students to their learning in a multidimensional manner.

Social networking and Facebook in particular can be helpful in illustrating the need for media literacy. Facebook developed virally; what was once the exclusive province of Harvard University is now globally accessible and regularly used. Yet while more people are making connections and communicating across space and time via Facebook, that increased communication does not mean we actually know any more about our interpersonal interactions or about the structures that make that increased communication possible. Facebook encourages an apolitical participation in civic space, but users can make the space political. The participants' talk about Facebook made clear that they have had little training in critical analysis of media texts, and their general belief that Facebook is ubiquitous and that to *not* have a Facebook presence is "weird" show they have internalized its ideological message: All information, including how to gather it and what deserves to be shared, should be publicly available. The participants labor for Facebook on a regular basis while believing that it is exclusively available for their personal enjoyment.

Social networking and particularly Facebook have eased the transition from high school or college and made geographic relocation easier by providing a secure (digital) place where one's long-term relationships can be protected. Facebook has helped make the shift from the familiar to the unfamiliar a less arduous experience. There must be a way to harness that perceived security to make schools operate more successfully. However, to get caught up in the trend or latest shift in Facebook is not helpful. Critical media literacy can analyze the popularity of Facebook as well as put it into a larger context.

At its most incisive, critical media literacy can draw from and share with the community. It can provide to both students and teachers a vocabulary and a set of strategies to approach their studies that connects classroom material with the larger environment. Students are taught a process of analytical inquiry that, at its most concrete, gives them ways to critique the media. More abstractly, it teaches them that, as citizens, they are a part of, not apart from, the larger environment in which they live, even when that environment actively rejects them. Based on the participant interviews throughout the text and now focusing on advice from Peter, Jacline, Stacey and Serenity to the next generation of students about to move from high school into college or work, it seems they want to be a part of authentic, experiential learning. They want to see the work done to improve schools and their experiences can be valuable guides. They want their schools and experiences with schooling to be better. How can that be made to happen?

Making Change

Peter: I miss the innocence of high school and I miss how easy it was. Some days, it's so easy to regret the decisions I made in life. And I could regret having gone to LSHS, and not taking it seriously and not doing my work the way I should have. But everything adds up to who you are, the mistakes you made make you who you are, make you stronger and you don't get to repeat those. I appreciate that I made all those mistakes at a young age.

As frustrated as he was by his high school, Peter nevertheless misses the innocence of those years compared with what he has learned in the intervening years. Peter believes he now takes his work more seriously *because* he was not serious in high school and then suffered for it when he got to college. He points out that change is difficult. Resisting the short-term lure of neoliberalism is also difficult; to do so, our position on individuality needs to shift to one that values interdependence.

Reflecting on the infusion of the neoliberal ethos across the social structure, it becomes clear that the policies of the free market do not work for or on behalf of dispossessed youth. Evidence does show, however, that when crises occur, and when those most directly impacted by the crises are at their most vulnerable, policy makers focused on the prowess of the free market swoop in and make rapid, radical changes in the superficial name of altruism and improvement.[1] In so doing, they hide their larger profit-oriented agenda. Those already in positions of power garner greater power while those hampered by the system remain so.

When private industries open schools and then, in turn, create curricula for said schools, they effectively remove themselves from any interrogation. Because they are privately held, their work need not be transparent, nor must they be accountable to the public. Yes, more money is always helpful, but Race to the Top illustrates that *how* that extra money is spent needs clarification. Increased privatization of the public school system hobbles critical thinking because the private industries running schools actively close themselves off from critical inquiry or constructive criticism. Businesses working in the service of public industry, such as those invested in schooling and school reform, should be held publicly accountable.

Schools can do a solid job bettering a community by being *a part of*, not *apart from*, the community. When EMOs come into communities, the money they bring in does not stay in the community, whereas local money spent on schools stays local. As Harlem Children's Zone has illustrated, this is not a simple problem, and faced with ongoing challenges, especially in the schools, Geoffrey Canada opted for external funding (Tough 2008). The zone within which Canada operates is undoubtedly stronger in the short term because of the external funding, but it raises the question: Will the community benefit from the funding in the long term? When the external private funders find greater opportunities for financial growth elsewhere, will Harlem suffer? External funding is indeed hard to turn down, but if it is not accompanied by powerful measures to bolster from within, the communities receiving the funding will be left with more problems, not more successes. There is a way to prepare schools to be successful–keeping communities involved.

Preparation

Jacline: The advice I would give a city kid before they go away to college is that they should prepare themselves and get into a college work flow before choosing to go. They need to know the college routine, and what it takes to be a good college student. Make sure all bases are covered in terms of what a college student should know about college like financial aid, add/drop, time management, study habits, where on campus can I go to get help, etc. It would help to take some college courses while in high school, to do research and ask questions, also going to visit colleges before is a big help. Once there, it is a good idea to ask for help and ask questions no matter how small or how much you think it might not be important because it will help you make sense of things. I say this because these are the things I wished I knew before leaving home. My high school should have prepared me for this more and offered me more opportunities that would have let me explore what being a college student really was and what it felt like instead of just giving information and facts, and I believe all high school students should have these opportunities.

While President Obama (2009) has stated that all students should be prepared for college by high school graduation, this nebulous declaration means very little, especially when we look at Jacline's very practical advice. Jacline speaks about personal responsibility: "They" (the students) should prepare themselves. The day-to-day realities of college life include knowing practical data, time management, study habits and where to seek out help. As Peter commented in Chapter Five, there is no handholding in college. When neoliberalism makes individual choice and responsibility its primary public sentiment, it is easy to see Peter and Jacline's recommendations as evidence of neoliberalism's potency. However, what Jacline advises is for students to be aware of the system they are about to enter. Personal and systemic responsibility must work together. The political rhetoric of incentivized learning, competition between schools and students, performance pay for teachers, increased testing and accountability are phrases that do not necessarily translate to a student's actual experience. What Jacline explains, and what was evident in the participants' talk throughout this text, is that their high school did not provide adequate systemic knowledge. The students were made just aware enough of the expectations of larger society to see they were failing at them and had enough knowledge to know they were pathologized as deviant by the larger society. Jacline emphasizes the importance of learning how to ask questions; critical inquiry is an entry point to critical media literacy. When secondary school reform focuses on rote, formulaic learning, increased testing, and adherence to business models of information transactions, the process of critical inquiry is stunted.

Reflections on "preparation" are multivaried and shift over time. For example, one year out of high school, Bruce felt as if he had been well prepared, yet a year after that, when he was not making the progress he wanted, he struggled and believed that he had been ill prepared. This experience is representative of many New York City community college students: The reputation of the city community colleges is that they are extensions of high school, continuing to shuffle weaker students through the system. If this is the case, then Giroux's (2003, 2009b, 2010b) concerns about the pipeline to mediocre jobs or prison are probably true. The changes being made in primary and secondary schools are focused on increased privatization for global competition, which means that already privileged students will receive increased privileges while struggling students and communities will continue to falter, thereby setting these young people up for continued subjugation.

If competition is the objective, then all students, including those from dispossessed backgrounds, deserve high quality primary and secondary educations to prepare them for whatever choices they make beyond high school. This means that all students, even those deemed less promising, deserve adequate preparation, which includes multiple opportunities for broad-spectrum learning in high school and the chance to better make sense of what comes after high school. In fact, those from dispossessed communities deserve *better than* adequate education. If attending college is the goal, then college preparation needs to be part of the school curriculum from the moment school begins; the urban community college system, such as New York's, can no longer be simply an extension of high school.

One route of preparation is to make (or keep) schools a deeply integrated part of the community. The ideological work of school needs to be better understood: Strong schools make communities stronger only if they are part of the community, not part of a private, for-profit organization that operates separately from the community. Schools deserve to be treated as professional organizations, with teachers as professionals but not like businesses. The work of schools is fundamentally different from the work of business. Teachers are not products and students are not consumers. Individuals interested in becoming teachers deserve proper, comprehensive training. In Chapter One, I commented that people without degrees do not make medical decisions, yet with no training in education, the general public feels qualified to make pedagogical assertions. To extend the metaphor: No one would ever go to a doctor who had no medical training, yet people seem to have little difficulty sending children to classrooms led by teachers with no professional training. In the face of private industry takeover and charter school development, that is exactly what happens: Teachers in schools run by private industry do not need to follow standard models of preparation, so individuals with no formal pedagogical training may be in the front of the classroom. These inexperienced individuals (who, in their defense, might be looking to make positive change in impoverished communities) are hired *because of* their inexperience and lack of training in order to parrot the interests of private industry.

Current evidence demonstrates that what works in classrooms is strong, dedicated teachers.[2] To educate individuals to become strong, dedicated teachers means comprehensive schooling and training. To be adequately prepared for the realities of the 21st century classroom, teachers need a thorough education in their chosen subjects as well as in critical media literacy. As Darling-Hammond (2010) noted, teachers work to prepare students for an unknown future that will require as yet unknown skills. What *is* known is that the media continue to be a guiding socializing force in the intersecting environments of global economy, information and entertainment. It is necessary to critically approach the study of the media in classrooms, across curricula and subjects. Teachers need media literacy in order to make their classrooms relevant to 21st century demands and to keep up with their students' out-of-school learning. If private industry takes over public schooling, teachers' ability to develop critical inquiry (of any subject) will be seriously impaired. There is little space to proactively critique the funding source.

Keep Focused

Stacey: I would say to stay focused and remember what you are there for. It is important to have fun but don't get caught up in the college life, like not going to class but getting involved in all kinds of clubs, or going to every party. It is important to keep a balance. I wish they stressed the transition more from high school to college because some of the smarter students I knew flunked out their first semester. If there was some way they could have prepared us for that. I definitely feel that schools can do more to prepare students for college: First the work load and to be more strict on assignments and preparing us more for what professors will be like. And stressing how students write and our grammar. I was always good in high school English but in college, not so much.

Stacey's advice is as pertinent for first-term college students as it is for education reformers: Stay focused, remember what school is for, and strive for balance. For many young people, there are but a few months between high school and college, yet the constructed worlds of these two education institutions are markedly different. Stacey's wish that her high school had paid more attention to the transition between the two worlds suggests that schools and school reformers need to find their focus and move beyond rhetoric.

Current debates within education reform question the purpose of, and the content of, both secondary and university learning. The importance of school and schooling is generally accepted; it is more challenging to follow that with consensus on *why* school and schooling are important. Despite the absence of transparency, many people have fixed opinions on what makes a good student, a good teacher, a good school, a good college program. These opinions are often contradictory, and they produce factions that form irreconcilable well-protected barriers, secure in their distance from each other.[3] The current state of education reform has little focus and no balance.

The intervention of critical media literacy, with its focus on critical inquiry, can help disentangle these conflicting opinions while informing young people, teachers and families about the larger structures under which their individual school operates, as well as their guiding ethos. The United States does not need a single-model school system or a national curriculum—neither of these would be tenable, nor are they necessarily in the best interest of the public good or social justice. But the multiple organizing principles should be more transparent. Critical media literacy can work to peel away the opaque layers. Once again, this demonstrates the need for teacher training and a foundation of critical inquiry.

A "one-size-fits-all" model does not work in schooling, especially in a country with the geographic breadth of the United States. Despite its current economic problems, the American higher education system is lauded for its variety that includes community colleges, city and state universities, private liberal arts colleges, research institutes and the highly competitive Ivy League. In its ideal, the system provides options for every student and any interest. Singularity is promoted in secondary schools, whereas variety is promoted in higher learning. Generations of politicians have tried to create a singular template for the secondary public school system. The inclusion of "common standards and assessments" in the Race to the Top language implies a move towards a nationalized curriculum. While there should be common agreement among schools across the nation, it must also be recognized that communities across the nation differ from each other and deserve individualized attention. Primary and secondary school reform that attempts to make one template "work" for all students means that, once again, those already prepared for success will continue to succeed. Common assessments and standards are unlikely to originate from densely packed urban schools. As interpreted through Freire (1970/2000), those already struggling learn to accept their struggles rather than fight against them. When students and teachers do not succeed in this model, they, rather than the system, are blamed.

Start-up schools whose student body is made up of disenfranchised youth work within a system that is designed to fail them or at least keep them disenfranchised. The participants in this study repeatedly stated that they were not prepared for college. They focus on their school's interpersonal connections, its lack of attention to the realities of a full workload and its lack of opportunities for advanced or extracurricular learning. It is disturbing that they attended a school ostensibly focused on the media and yet learned little to no critical analysis as evidenced by their general lack of critiques of Facebook and their complacent distance from larger civic issues. For example, Nino complained about the absence of opportunity in the school. A smart, capable young woman, Nino felt lost after high school and did not like the way classes were taught in the local community college in New York City or in the state school in California. What might have been different if Nino had been able to choose from a range of courses in high school? Admittedly, small schools have smaller budgets and cannot afford to offer many choices, but in a building housing six other schools in addition to LSHS, why must the schools operate in isolation from each other? What are the implications when students are all shuffled into the same building, then told to remain completely separate from their peers? If nothing else, this reinforces a compartmentalized learning that encourages individual progression without community support. Young people are taught that the route to success is a solo journey, and if they stumble along the way, that is their own responsibility. Operating within such strict (and also unclear) confines, Nino is left frustrated.

Critical inquiry does not immediately produce better schools, better communities or better teachers. However, it does result in a more thoroughly informed populace, aware of its interdependence, reliant on the burden of individual freedom and responsibility. Dispossessed communities will not flourish overnight because of critical media literacy, but critical media literacy exposes at once the rhetoric of reform. Young people from impoverished communities deserve more than rhetoric. Private industry and politicians invest in results that do not necessarily coalesce with the results desired by students, teachers and their families. This study reveals both an underlying fear and complacency: Participants who fear they will not be successful (a rational fear, given the messages they receive from the larger society) behave in a complacent manner, insuring their position as docile bodies in menial labor. Critical media literacy may flip the narrative, showing students how their participation intersects with the larger culture.

The participants in this study felt ill prepared for life after high school. It is a perpetually challenging task for a school to keep its focus in helping young people prepare for the future. Popcorn is aware that literature is not a "practical" major, but one that teaches him how to think critically and communicate effectively, and he observes that this will help him in any career choice. Instead of falling prey to the whims of the market, schools need to focus on the broad range of skills young people will need for the future.

Not all students flunk out of college because they are engaging in risky behavior free from the direct supervision of a parent/guardian. As Stacey observed, and Genevieve's experience demonstrated, some smart students flunk out because they are unprepared to balance freedom and responsibility. College crystallizes many of the social and economic disparities of adolescence. Having been shuffled through secondary school, or rewarded for nonacademic successes, they do not know how to negotiate the adjustments necessary in college. Participants in this study continually asked for greater boundaries in schooling: Stricter adherence to deadlines, greater attention to the impact of their work, greater attention to their abilities to balance multiple tasks simultaneously. Despite changes in technology, fundamental skills such as writing, continue to be important. What is "good" in high school is not necessarily adequate in college, and what is exemplary at one college is not necessarily acceptable at another. As Peter laments, his 3.8 GPA at community college was not deemed valuable at a competitive liberal arts college. As part of preparing young people to be competitive individuals, schools need to focus on what matters in the short as well as the long term. Technology skills are indeed important, as is the ability to approach problems critically, speak about them coherently and write about them clearly. Schools these days operate from a place of apprehension that works its way into students' learning. If young people continue to be educated in such an environment, will they learn to fear the future? If so, will they lack the confidence necessary to take risks that might develop a critically aware, competitive workforce?

Take (Responsible) Risks

Serenity: I think a city kid should go away to college, get a sense of freedom and the college experience. However, I would let them know: Before you go to college, please know who you are and be content with yourself, because when you don't know yourself there will be a lot of people in college who will play off your vulnerability and innocence. You have to be set in who you are and don't change just because you're in college. If you do happen to change, let it be ABOUT GROWTH. Don't change negatively!

It must be asked: Why is it that, absent critical knowledge, massive changes in education and the media can be made without the degree of self-awareness that Serenity believes important? The rapid changes proposed in education are not sustainable. If individual change should be about growth, then so should systemic change.

Including critical media literacy across curricula is a risk. It cannot be "tested" in any traditional, known, standardized manner. It challenges the teacher-student hierarchy. It brings potentially controversial pop culture texts into the classroom. It may dissolve the classroom/nonclassroom learning barriers. It slows down the learning process with its attention to detail, analysis and continued inquiry. It is a risk that connects individual to institution. At its most basic, critical media literacy invites young people, teachers and families to critically analyze a slew of texts. There is no one, single codified approach to media literacy in the United States,[4] and the evidence of the divisive potency of neoliberalism is that it is rare for multiple organizations to be in conversation with each other. I opened this text advocating for the inclusion of critical media without clearly explaining what, beyond the equally vague "critical inquiry," I mean. The multiple processes under the umbrella "media literacy" have different emphases, techniques of analysis, textual emphases and placement in the classroom/community.[5] All scholars concerned with improving and growing media literacy curricula broadly agree that greater formal attention to the media is needed. They agree that young people should develop skills for critically analyzing the media and become involved in media production so they may experience and make sense of how a text is produced.[6] As advocacy in favor of critical media literacy and against the ethos of neoliberalism, the multiple techniques are interdependent, not individually operating. Instead of detailing what style of critical media literacy to follow, I encourage the following steps–risks that must be taken in order to alter the stories told by the next generation of high school graduates:

- *Teacher training in media literacy*

  Primary and secondary school teachers deserve professional development opportunities in media literacy. Individuals who enter education schools or train to be teachers are highly encouraged to seek out courses in media criticism if their schools do not offer specific media literacy courses.

  Media education should be part of the primary and secondary school curricula, but without teacher training and, ultimately, teacher certification in media literacy, there are not nearly enough qualified people to grow the discipline. Teachers interested in including the study and application of media in their classes often do so on their own, with little support. Young people know a great deal about the mainstream mass media, often more than their teachers. They can access information independently of their classroom learning, but they do not necessarily possess the formal skills of analysis that media literacy offers. Teachers should not shoulder the responsibility of teaching this without having had training and professional development.

• *Continued codification of the multiple, intersecting and sometimes oppositional efforts being made in media literacy in the United States and across the globe*

The multiple definitions of media literacy and media education in the United States are indicative of a conflicted relationship with the media. The definitions and motivations of the media should continue to be debated in public forums as a way to make the field as rich and as thoroughly explored as possible. There is no one-size-fits-all in education and there certainly is no one-size-fits-all model in media literacy. However, practical work needs to get done and especially in the era of digital information sharing, practical work is relatively easy to access if teachers/scholars/researchers know what to look for. To enable the most productive work that aligns with a classroom or school's goals, there should be a clear review of who is doing what, and with what intent, in the broad field of media literacy/media education.[7] Primary and secondary teachers searching for training and education opportunities deserve a clear set of directions in order to implement the most valuable work in their classrooms. Media education should remain complex and multidimensional, but it should not be too complicated to access.

• *Continued research on the efficacy of media literacy learning*

This is a two-fold need: increased research on the application of media education in classrooms to have a better idea of what works as well as development of standards of evaluation and assessment so that students can monitor their progress.

In order to make media literacy matter to teachers and in classrooms, there must be more research on the efficacy and quality of work in media education. Increased participant-observation and ethnographic work is needed to see and make sense of what work is being done, and with what goals and outcomes. Advocates of media education must have at hand the necessary evidence that what they are doing matters.

Media literacy skills may not be tested by any common standard, but assessment in some form is necessary so students can observe their own knowledge development. This includes work on self-reflection, textual analysis, production and application of key terminology. This work does not fit into a standardized test model though, and thus this implies a re-evaluation of tools of assessment.

The 20 participants in this study are complex, complicated individuals faced with a host of social, political and economic obstacles. They received a subpar high school education, in part because the accident of their economic situation is replicated time and again within a neoliberal environment that values individual choice and competition without systemic support. In a way, the failure of the education system is intentional: It keeps these young people docile and maneuvers them along the pipeline of subservience and subjugation. Their individual teachers and their school did the best job they could, but unable to rise above the environment where it was situated, the school was systemically arranged to fail the students. Some of the students replicate that model: By rejecting college, regardless of the obvious flaws of the university system, these young people have almost guaranteed their continued dispossession. Some know that college is the most direct (traditional) route to a successful professional life. However, in large part because of an achievement gap that set them back at a young age, they attend community or vocational colleges that catch them up rather than push them forward. A few possess intangible skills that help them maneuver through the system in more proactive, productive ways, with a great deal of hard work and dedication. All participants know their success or failure is based on their hard work *and* a readily available support system.

Underserved urban youth are raised in an environment of trepidation engendered by generations of struggle. They learn to avoid certain (intellectual) risk-taking activities and simultaneously learn that society fears them. Through the overlapping lenses of postfeminism and neoliberalism, they receive the confusing message that certain young people can do anything they desire. Not them, though—not poor young people of color, who remain on the fringes because they cannot adequately compete in a consumer-based, free-market environment.

Socioeconomically struggling youth have more pertinent needs than critical media literacy. Invoking the theory behind Geoffrey Canada's Harlem Children's Zone, they need a whole environment that supports their growth. This whole is made up of multiple parts, and my part, as a media literacy scholar and practitioner, is to advocate for media education: Young people, their teachers and their families need critical media literacy skills in order to secure their own individual growth as well as to contribute to the growth of their local communities and the global community.

APPENDIX: PARTICIPANTS

Name	Ethnicity	Gender	Year of HS graduation	College/ Work	Private/ Public/ Community	Switched Schools?
Brick	White	Male	2010	College	Private	No
Bruce*	African American	Male	2008	College	Community	No
Genevieve*	African American	Female	2009	College	Private, Community	Yes
Hass	Latino	Male	2010	Work		
Helena	Latina	Female	2010	College	Private	No
Jacline	Latina	Female	2008	College	Public (state), Public (city)	Yes
Jasmine	Asian	Female	2008	College	Private	No
John	Latino	Male	2010	Work		
Johnny	Asian	Male	2008	Work		
Last	Latino	Male	2008	College	Community	No
Lucy*	Latina	Female	2009	Work		
Natalie	Latina	Female	2008	College	Community	No
Nino*	Latina	Female	2008	Work		
Peter*	African American	Male	2008	College	Community, Private	Yes
Pink	Latina	Female	2010	Work		
Planet J	African American	Male	2008	College	Community	
Popcorn*	African American	Male	2008	College	Public	
Serenity	African American	Female	2009	College	Private, Public	Yes
Snapper	African American	Male	2009	College	Public, Vocational	Yes
Stacey*	African American	Female	2009	College	Private	No

* Participants who also participated in research for Butler, *Media Education Goes to School* (2010)

|NOTES

Introduction

1 All proper names and some identifying details have been changed to protect the confidentiality of participants. Participants chose their own code names.

2 See Hall & Jefferson (1976); Hebdige (1979); McRobbie (1976); Willis (1977).

3 See Appendix for table of participants, their demographic data and their post-high school academic/work choices and changes.

4 boyd (2007b); boyd & Ellison (2007); Ross, Orr, Sisic, Arsenault, Simmering & Orr (2009); Tufekci (2008).

5 Giroux (2009b; 2010b); Saltman (2002; 2005; 2007a; 2007b).

6 Klein (2007); Harvey (1999; 2005; 2010); Saltman (2005; 2007a).

7 Giroux (2009a; 2010a); Harvey (2010).

8 For incisive critique of the connection between neoliberalism and socioeconomically struggling communities, see Saltman (2007a; 2010).

9 Auletta (2011); Grossman (2010); Vargas (2010).

10 Institutional names and some geographic locations have been changed or removed to protect confidentiality.

11 boyd (2007b; 2009; 2010); boyd & Ellison (2007); Butler (2011).

12 See the development of his writing on neoliberalism and schooling: Friedman (1995; 2002; 2005).

13 Giroux (2009a; 2009b; 2010a, 2010b); Harvey (1999; 2005); Klein (2007); Saltman (2005; 2007a; 2007b).

Chapter One

1 Detailed analyses of Harlem Children's Zone and Geoffrey Canada's work can be found in Canada (2010); Guggenheim (2010); Tough (2008).

2 For detailed discussions of particular schools and/or school systems, see Alonso, Anderson, Su & Theoharis (2009); Ancess & Allen (2006); Butler (2010); Podair (2002); Ravitch (1974/2000; 2010); Ripley (2008); Saltman (2005).

3 Discussions of specific reforms can be found in Ancess & Allen (2006); Daniels (2009); Hanushek (2010); Matthews (2009); Tough (2008); Tyner-Mullings (2008).
4 Ancess & Allen (2006); Bracey (2002); Hanushek (2010); Miron & Applegate (2007).
5 For specific and overlapping critiques on education as job training, see Ayers (2009); Giroux
   (2009b; 2010a); Leistyna (2007); Saltman (2005; 2007b).
6 Ayers (2009); Saltman (2005; 2007a; 2007b).
7 Faculty are not immune to political changes in their universities. Faculty work is increasingly af-
   fected by pressure to perform in order to make money for their respective schools and to prepare
   students for the workforce. See Giroux (2009b; 2010a); Searls-Giroux (2008–2009) and Martin
   (2008–2009) for scorching critiques of depleted academic freedoms in the face of corporatizing
   higher education. This shift will undoubtedly influence teaching. Robert Jensen (2011) refers
   to himself as a "provider of educational products to consumers" and warns that the result will
   be "the end of real education, if by education we mean independent inquiry into the power that
   structures our lives" (theobserver.com).
8 Arnett (2004); Bloom (2005); Taylor (2010).
9 Whether they can afford it or not, Americans are aware that college comes with significant costs.
   Until recently, this was not the case in the United Kingdom, where students generally attended
   university free of charge. In a special issue of *Culture Machine* (2010) devoted to the implications of tuition charged for university education, several scholars predict disaster. Though the
   economic implications in the U.K. are different than in the U.S, it is useful to consider the
   predictions and concerns of scholars who see the academy on the brink of monumental change.
   Couldry and McRobbie (2010) argue that "over the long term, the range of degrees most universities offer will be narrowed" in part because if university finances are supported by promises of
   future earnings, degrees in liberal arts and humanities will dwindle. Overall, the authors believe
   that what is under threat is the advancement of critical thinking, intellectual development and
   creative potential, irrespective of family wealth. See especially Rovito's 'On the Death of the
   University,' Sidorenko's 'Education, Education, Education,' Manghani's 'Amidst the Culture of
   Efficiency' and Lockwood's 'Our Miners Moment: The Battle to Save Higher Education for
   Working Class Students' (culturemachine.net).
10 See Menard Live and Learn (2011) for his review of Richard Arum and Josipa Roksa's *Academically Adrift* and Professor X's (a pseudonym) *In the Basement of the Ivory Tower.*
11 Ayers (2009); Darling-Hammond (2009); Gillen (2009).
12 Any union an individual might belong to from a previous teaching position has no bargaining
   or grievance privileges in charter schools.
13 For detailed analyses and discussions of these debates, see Bracey (2002) for discussion of charter
   schools' war on public schools and the standards of accountability; Bulkley (2004) and Payne
   & Knowles (2009) for discussion of charter school autonomy; Buckley & Schneider (2007)
   for analyses of autonomy and absence of evidence of charter school efficacy; Miron & Nelson
   (2004) for discussion of autonomy; Ravitch (2010) for a broad history of charter schools as well
   as detailed critiques of the evidence of their efficacy; Wells (2002) for analyses of charter school
   start-up and maintenance; Miron & Applegate (2007) for discussion of teacher attrition in charter schools; Fuller, Gawlick, Kuboyama-Gonzales & Park (2004) for analyses of the concept of
   "choice" and private organization.
14 For discussion of the early development of Race to the Top in the popular press, see Christensen
   & Horn (2009); Cruz (2009; 2010); Dillon (2010a). For early government language and development, see US Department of Education (2009).
15 See also Dillon, *Education Grant Effort Faces Late Opposition* (2010a).
16 Darling-Hammond (2010); Miller (2003); Ripley (2010).

Chapter Two

1 See especially boyd (2007b; 2010); Glaeser (2010); Tufekci (2008); Turkle (2011).
2 Especially helpful are Fine (1998); Fine & Sandstrom (1988); Guba & Lincoln (1998); Schwandt
   (1998).

3   For constructions of self on Facebook, see boyd (2010); boyd & Ellison (2007). For constructing portraits of participants in qualitative research, see Fine (1998); Heldke (1998).
4   See Hall (1992) for his discussion of Angela McRobbie's vital inclusion of feminism in cultural studies.
5   See boyd (2010); Schofield-Clark (2008); Turkle (2011).
6   For discussion on how social networking is used by young people, see boyd (2007a; 2010); Tufekci (2008); Turkle (2011). On how teachers use social networking to better connect with students, see Long (2010); Lipton (2011). For discussion on social networking's integral role in digital and technological development, see Morozov (2011); Siegel (2008); Turkle (2011).
7   Six additional people agreed to be participants, then never followed up on repeated requests for interviews. We continue to stay in touch as "regular" Facebook friends. My interpretation is that they were interested in the process but unable or unwilling to make the time for the work involved. One person let me know that because of his travels he would not be on his computer for months at a time and did not want to harm my process.
8   All information on Facebook cited from Facebook.com accurate as of August 2011.
9   There is a Facebook page with 1183 "likes" titled "I remember when Sconex was poppinnn!"
10 For detailed popular press coverage of the development of Facebook, see Grossman (2010); Miller (2010); Vargas (2010). For scholarly work on Facebook, including its history, see boyd (2007a); Tufekci (2008); Walther, VanDerHeide, Kim, Westerman & Tong (2008). See also Facebook's own published statistics on their webpage, facebook.com.
11 Facebook.com (2011) *Facebook & Skype*; *Timeline*.
12 See Buckingham (2000), Giroux (2009b) and Projansky (2007) for discussion of the construction of young people as social problems.
13 For contrasting data on the debate about how young people operate and are approached on the Internet, see Hoffman (2010); Parker-Pope (2011); Richtel (2011); Bazelon (2011); Glaeser (2010); McNamara (2006); Rich (2007).
14 For discussion of Facebook and privacy, see Auletta (2011); Brustein (2010); Harrell (2011); Miller (2010).
15 Google, the Internet's largest traditional indexer, is threatened by Facebook's presence and power, and by June 2011 it had made a focused effort to enter its orbit, launching Google+, a social network site focused on sharing with like-minded groups rather than individuals. For early discussion of Google+ see Auletta (2011); Miller (2011).
16 Bruce, Nino, Genevieve, Popcorn, Peter, Lucy and Stacey were all participants whose stories appeared in *Media Education Goes to School*.
17 For discussion see Bazelon (2011); Hoffman (2010); Parker-Pope (2011); Paul (2010); Richtel (2010).
18 See Bazelon (2011); Glaeser (2010); McNamara (2006).
19 For a more thorough exploration of Nino, her graphic design business and her use of Facebook, see: Butler "'I just gotta get this business started!': Understanding young women and business through a case study of a young entrepreneur" (forthcoming).

Chapter Four
1   Regents are the New York State assessment tests, taken periodically from 8th to 12th grade. Students need to pass a series of tests in basic subjects with a minimum score of 55 in order to graduate with a traditional high school diploma. Students may retake the Regents, offered in fall and spring, as many times as necessary to pass.
2   Gladwell (2010); Parker (2011); Vargas (2011).

Chapter Five
1   See especially Ancess & Allen (2006); Bracey (2002); Buckley & Schneider (2007); Bulkley (2004); Fuller et al. (2004); Ravitch (2010); Wells (2002).

Chapter Seven

1 Giroux (2003; 2010a; 2010b); Leistyna (2007); Saltman (2005; 2007a).
2 See Darling-Hammond (2010); Ripley (2010); Weingarten (2010).
3 See Menard's Live and Learn (2011), especially his debate about the purpose of college and his review of research on what is learned in college. See also Weber's reader *Waiting for "Superman"* (2010), with essays from sometimes contradictory positions on how to improve secondary schooling.
4 See especially the Action Coalition for Media Education (ACME, actioncoalition.org), The Media Education Foundation (MEF, mediaed.org) and the Partnership for 21st Century Skills (p21.org) for non-corporate-funded work in media education. When corporations fund media literacy initiatives, or when individual scholars accept corporate funding, one should treat them with caution.
5 My own research and work in media education is informed primarily by David Buckingham. See especially Buckingham's *Media Education* (2003) for a detailed discussion of the changes in media and the social construction of childhood that frames his argument on the necessity of media education. This text also details the four concepts of media education and how to apply those concepts to classroom learning.
6 This happens with a great deal of variety and some remarkably contradictory methods. The Media Education Lab at Temple University (mediaeducationlab.com), for example, has little in common with the work done through the Media Education Foundation (mediaed.org), yet both operate under the title "media education," and both subscribe to the belief that media literacy/ media education is important. In the United States especially, there is little that is agreed upon in *what* and *how* to teach young people about the media.
7 See Domaille and Buckingham (2001) for a map of work being done across the globe in media education, including conflicting views/methods within certain countries.

WORKS CITED

Alonso, G., Anderson, N. S., Su, C., & Theoharis, J. (2009). *Our schools suck: Students talk back to a segregated nation on the failures of urban education.* New York: NYU Press.

Anastasia. (August 19, 2008). R.I.P. Sconex. *YPulse.* Retrieved August 4, 2011, from ypulse.com/rip-sconex.

Ancess, J., & Allen, D. (2006). Implementing small theme high schools in New York City: Great intentions and great tensions. *Harvard Educational Review, 76*(3), 401–416.

Anderson, N. (September 25, 2009). Unions criticize Obama's school proposals as "Bush III." *Common Dreams.* Retrieved February 17, 2010, from commondreams.org.

Arnett, J.J. (2004). *Emerging adulthood: The winding road from the late teens through the twenties.* Oxford: Oxford University Press.

Auletta, K. (July 11 & 18, 2011). A woman's place: Can Sheryl Sandberg upend Silicon Valley's male-dominated culture? *The New Yorker,* 54–63.

Ayers, B., & Klonsky, M. (2007). Disaster politics and the right-wing assault on public schooling and public space: A dialogue between Bill Ayers and Mike Klonsky. In K. J. Saltman (Ed.), *Schooling and the politics of disaster* (pp. 177–188). New York: Routledge.

Ayers, W. (Summer 2009). Barack Obama and the fight for public education. *Harvard Educational Review, 79*(2), 385–395.

Banchero, S. (January 11, 2011). School changes pushed by Rhee. *The Wall Street Journal.* Retrieved February 13, 2011, from wsj.com.

Bazelon, E. (June 26, 2011). The ninny state. *The New York Times.* Retrieved June 27, 2011, from nytimes.com.

Bloom, J. L. (2005). Hollowing the promises of higher education: Inside the political economy of access to college. In L. Weis & M. Fine (Eds.), *Beyond silenced voices: Class, race and gender in United States schools* (pp. 63–81). New York: SUNY Press.

boyd, d. (May 18, 2007a). *Digital handshakes on virtual receiving lines.* Paper presented at the Personal Democracy Forum, New York, NY.

boyd, d. (2007b). Why youth (heart) social network sites: The role of networked publics in teenage social life. In D. Buckingham (Ed.), *Youth, identity and digital media: The MacArthur Foundation series on digital learning*. Cambridge, MA: MIT Press.

boyd, d. (February 26, 2009). *Social media is here to stay…now what?* Paper presented at the Microsoft Research TechFest, Redmond, WA.

boyd, d. (October 23, 2010). *Living life in public: Why American teens choose publicity over privacy.* Paper presented at the Association of Internet Researchers, Gothenburg, Sweden.

boyd, d., & Ellison, N. (2007). Social network sites: Definition, history and scholarship. *Computer-Mediated Communication, 12*(1), article 11. Avail: jcmc.indiana.edu.

Bracey, G. W. (2002). *The war against America's public schools: Privatizing schools, commercializing education*. Boston: Allyn & Bacon.

Brooks, D. (October 23, 2009). The quiet revolution. *The New York Times*. Retrieved November 12, 2009, from nytimes.com.

Brown, R. (October 3, 2008). Crusader of the classrooms. *The Atlantic*. Retrieved January 12, 2010, from theatlantic.com.

Brustein, J. (May 12, 2010). Is there life after Facebook? *The New York Times*. Retrieved February 13, 2011, from nytimes.com.

Buckingham, D. (2000). *After the death of childhood: Growing up in the age of electronic media*. London: Polity Press.

Buckingham, D. (2003). *Media education: Literacy, learning and contemporary culture*. London: Polity Press.

Buckley, J., & Schneider, M. (2007). *Charter schools: Hope or hype?* Princeton, NJ: Princeton University Press.

Bulkley, K. E. (2004). Balancing act: Educational management organizations and charter school autonomy. In K. E. Bulkley & P. Wohlstetter (Eds.), *Taking account of charter schools: What's happened and what's next?* (pp. 121–141). New York: Teachers College Press.

Burns, F. (May 31, 2011). Driving away the best teachers. *The New York Times*. Retrieved May 31, 2011, from nytimes.com.

Butler, A. (2010). *Media education goes to school: Young people make meaning of media and urban education*. New York: Peter Lang.

Butler, A. (2011). Engaging Facebook: Making Facebook matter in the classroom. *Ubiquitous Learning Journal, 3*(3), 51–60.

Butler, A. (forthcoming). "I just gotta get this business started!": Understanding young women and business through a case study of a young entrepreneur. In M. Bae & O. Ivashkevich (Eds.), *Girls' Culture Anthology*. New York: Peter Lang.

Canada, G. (March 14, 2010). Schools are for kids, not adults. *New York Times*. Retrieved March 16, 2010, from nytimes.com.

Christensen, C. M., & Horn, M. B. (August 12, 2009). Revolution in the classroom. *The Atlantic*. Retrieved November 12, 2010, from theatlantic.com.

Corrigan, P., & Frith, S. (1976). The politics of youth culture. In S. Hall & T. Jefferson (Eds.), *Resistance through rituals* (pp. 231–239). London: Routledge.

Cotten, S. R., Anderson, W. A., & Tufekci, Z. (2009). Old wine in new technology or a different type of digital divide? *New Media and Society, 11*(7), 1163–1186.

Couldry, N., & McRobbie, A. (2010). The death of the university, English style. *Culture Machine*. Retrieved December 1, 2010, from culturemachine.net.

Cruz, G. (September 14, 2009). Can Arne Duncan (and $5 billion) fix America's schools? *Time*. Retrieved February 17, 2010, from time.com.

Cruz, G. (February 22, 2010). A quick fix for America's worst schools. *Time*. Retrieved February 17, 2010, from time.com.

Daniels, M. L. (Fall 2009). The three Fs of classroom management. *AASA Journal of Scholarship and Practice, 6*(3), 18–24.

Darling-Hammond, L. (Summer 2009). President Obama and education: The possibility for dramatic improvements in teaching and learning. *Harvard Educational Review, 79*(2), 210–223.

Darling-Hammond, L. (2010). *The flat world and education: How America's commitment to equity will determine our future*. New York: Teachers College Press.

Darling-Hammond, L. (May 30, 2011). A dangerous obsession. *The New York Times*. Retrieved May 30, 2011, from nytimes.com.

Delgado, A. (Summer 2009). Barack Obama for my education. *Harvard Educational Review, 79*(2), 225–226.

De Leon, B. (1996). Career development of Hispanic adolescent girls. In B. J. R. Leadbeater & N. Way (Eds.), *Urban girls: Resisting stereotypes, creating identities* (pp. 380–393). New York: NYU Press.

Dillon, S. (November 11, 2009a). States compete for federal school dollars. *The New York Times*. Retrieved November 12, 2009, from nytimes.com.

Dillon, S. (November 12, 2009b). After criticism, the administration is praised for final rules on education grants. *The New York Times*. Retrieved November 12, 2009, from nytimes.com.

Dillon, S. (January 19, 2010a). Education grant effort faces late opposition. *The New York Times*. Retrieved January 19, 2010, from nytimes.com.

Dillon, S. (February 1, 2010b). Obama to seek sweeping change in "no child" law. *The New York Times*. Retrieved February 1, 2010, from nytimes.com.

Dillon, S. (March 13, 2010c). Obama calls for major change in education. *The New York Times*. Retrieved March 16, 2010, from nytimes.com.

Dillon, S. (June 27, 2011). Teacher grades: Pass or be fired. *The New York Times*. Retrieved June 28, 2011, from nytimes.com.

Domaille, K., & Buckingham, D. (2001). *Youth media education survey*. UNESCO. Retrieved May 14, 2009 from http://portal.unesco.org.

Dominus, S. (December 6, 2010). Leader from different world visits classrooms. *The New York Times*. Retrieved December 6, 2010, from nytimes.com.

Ehrenreich, B. (September 11, 2007). College students, welcome to a lifetime of debt! *Alternet*. Retrieved June 21, 2011, from alternet.com.

Emmerich, R. (Director) (2009). *2012*.

Facebook & Skype. *Facebook*. Retrieved August 4, 2011, from facebook.com/skype.

Fertig, B. (November 12, 2009). Rules for Race to the Top funds could hurt NY. *WNYC*. Retrieved November 12, 2009, from wnyc.org.

Fincher, D. (Director) (2010). *The social network*.

Fine, G. A., & Sandstrom, K. L. (1988). *Knowing children: Participant observation with minors*. Newbury Park, CA: Sage.

Fine, M. (1998). Working the hyphens: Reinventing self and other in qualitative research. In N. K. Denzin & Y. S. Lincoln (Eds.), *The landscape of qualitative research* (pp. 130–155). Thousand Oaks, CA: Sage.

Freire, P. (1970/2000). *The pedagogy of the oppressed*. New York: Continuum Publishers.

Friedman, M. (1955). The role of government in education. Retrieved May 28, 2009, from school-choices.org.

Friedman, M. (1995). Public schools: Make them private. Retrieved May 28, 2009, from cato.org

Friedman, M. (July 2, 2002). The market can transform our schools. *New York Times*. Retrieved May 25 2009, from nytimes.com.

Friedman, M. (June 9, 2005). Free to choose. *The Wall Street Journal*. Retrieved May 28, 2009, from opinionjournal.com.

Fromme, K., Corbin, W. R., & Kruse, M. I. (2008). Behavioral risks during the transition from high school to college. *Developmental Psychology, 44*(5), 1497–1504.

Fuller, B., Gawlik, M., Kuboyama-Gonzales, E., & Park, S. (2004). Localized ideas of fairness: Inequality among charter schools. In K. E. Bulkley & P. Wohlstetter (Eds.), *Taking account of charter schools: What's happened and what's next?* (pp. 93–120). New York: Teachers College Press.

Geertz, C. (1983). *Local knowledge: Further essays in interpretive anthropology*. New York: Basic Books.

Gillen, J. (Summer 2009). An insurrectionary generation: Young people, poverty, education and Obama. *Harvard Educational Review, 79*(2), 363–369.

Giroux, H. (2003). *The abandoned generation: Democracy beyond the culture of fear.* New York: Palgrave Macmillan.

Giroux, H. (Summer 2009a). Obama's dilemma: Postpartisan politics and the crisis of American education. *Harvard Educational Review, 79*(2), 250–266.

Giroux, H. (2009b). *Youth in a suspect society: Democracy or disposability?* New York: Palgrave Macmillan.

Giroux, H. (2010a). Public values, higher education and the scourge of neoliberalism. *Culture Machine.* Retrieved December 1, 2010, from culturemachine.net.

Giroux, H. (2010b). Youth in dark times: Broken promises and dashed hopes. *The Culture Machine.* Retrieved December 1, 2010, from culturemachine.net.

Giroux, H., & Saltman, K. (December 17, 2008). Obama's betrayal of public education? Arne Duncan and the corporate model of schooling. *Truthout.* Retrieved February 17, 2008, from truthout.org.

Gladwell, M. (October 4, 2010). Small change: Why the revolution will not be tweeted. *The New Yorker.* Retrieved February 13, 2011, from newyorker.com.

Glaeser, E. L. (November 2, 2010). No man is an island. *The New York Times.* Retrieved February 13, 2011, from nytimes.com.

Goffman, E. (1959). *The presentation of self in everyday life.* New York: Anchor Books.

Green, E. (March 7, 2010). Building a better teacher. *The New York Times.* Retrieved March 7, 2010, from nytimes.com.

Greenhouse, S., & Dillon, S. (March 7, 2010). School's shake-up is embraced by the president. *The New York Times.* Retrieved March 7, 2010, from nytimes.com.

Grossman, L. (December 15, 2010). Mark Zuckerberg. *Time.* Retrieved February 13, 2011, from time.com.

Guba, E. G., & Lincoln, Y. S. (1998). Competing paradigms in qualitative research. In N. K. Denzin & Y. S. Lincoln (Eds.), *The landscape of qualitative research* (pp. 195–220). Thousand Oaks, CA: Sage.

Guggenheim, D. (Director) (2010). *Waiting for "Superman."*

Hall, S. (1992). Cultural studies and its theoretical legacies. In L. Grossberg, C. Nelson & P. Treichler (Eds.), *Cultural studies* (pp. 277–286). New York: Routledge.

Hall, S. & Jefferson, T. (Eds.) (1976). *Resistance through rituals.* London: Routledge.

Hanushek, E. (2010). The difference is great teachers. In K. Weber (Ed.), *Waiting for "Superman": How we can save America's failing public schools* (pp. 81–100). New York: Public Affairs.

Harrell, K. (February 11, 2011). Facebook: A spiritual experience? *The Huffington Post.* Retrieved February 13, 2011, from huffingtonpost.com.

Harvey, D. (1999). *The limits to capital.* London: Verso.

Harvey, D. (2005). *A brief history of neoliberalism.* Oxford: Oxford University Press.

Harvey, D. (2010). *The enigma of capital and the crises of capitalism.* Oxford: Oxford University Press.

Hebdige, D. (1979). *Subcultures: The meaning of style.* London: Routledge.

Heldke, L. (1998). On being a responsible traitor: A primer. In B. Bar-On & A. Ferguson (Eds.), *Daring to be good: Essays in feminist ethico-politics* (pp. 87–99). London: Routledge.

Herszenhorn, D. M. (December 18, 2010). Senate blocks bill for young illegal immigrants. *The New York Times.* Retrieved August 10, 2011, from nytimes.com

Hoffman, J. (December 4, 2010). As bullies go digital, parents play catch-up. *The New York Times.* Retrieved February 13, 2011, from nytimes.com.

Hu, W. (February 9, 2012). 10 states are given waivers from education law. *The New York Times.* Retrieved February 9, 2012, from nytimes.com.

Jensen, R. (May 2, 2011). Delivering educational products: The job formerly known as teaching. *The Observer.* Retrieved May 2, 2011, from theobserver.com.

Jones, S. (September 15, 2002). The Internet goes to college: How students are living in the future with today's technology. Retrieved March 31, 2011, from pewinternet.org.

Jones, S., & Fox, S. (January 2009). Generations online in 2009: Pew Internet and American Life Project. Retrieved March 31, 2011, from pewinternet.org.

Kearney, M. C. (2006). *Girls make media*. New York: Routledge.

Klein, N. (2007). *The shock doctrine: The rise of disaster capitalism*. New York: Metropolitan Books.

Kohn, A. (December 10, 2008). Beware school 'reformers.' *The Nation*. Retrieved February 18, 2010, from thenation.com.

Leistyna, P. (2007). No corporation left behind. In K. J. Saltman (Ed.), *Schooling and the politics of disaster* (pp. 141–157). New York: Routledge.

Lewin, T. (January 26, 2011). Record level of stress found in college freshmen. *The New York Times*. Retrieved February 13, 2011, from nytimes.com.

Lindlof, T. R. (1995). *Qualitative communication research methods*. Thousand Oaks,CA: Sage.

Lipton, M. (2011). Facebook as a functional tool and critical resource. In R. T. Scholz (Ed.), *Learning through digital media: Experiments in technology and pedagogy*. Retrieved April 14, 2011, from learningthroughdigitalmedia.net.

Lockwood, A. (2010). Our miners' moment: The battle to save higher education for working class students. *Culture Machine*. Retrieved December 1, 2010, from culturemachine.net.

Long, C.P. (December 2010). Cultivating communities of learning with digital media: Comparative education through blogging and podcasting. *Teaching Philosophy, 33*(4), 347–362.

Manghani, S. (2010). Amidst the culture of efficiency. *Culture Machine*. Retrieved December 1, 2010, from culturemachine.net.

Martin, R. (2008–2009). W(h)ither academic freedom? Revaluing faculty work. *Works and Days, 26&27*, 371–388. Retrieved June 21, 2011, from worksanddays.net.

Matgouranis, C., & Robe, J. (December 20, 2010). Is America saturated with college grads? *Forbes*. Retrieved December 20, 2010, from forbes.com.

Mathews, J. (2009). *Work hard, be nice: How two inspired teachers created the most promising schools in America*. Chapel Hill, NC: Algonquin Books.

McCabe, K. (January 24, 2010). Teen's suicide prompts a look at bullying. *The Boston Globe*. Retrieved January 24, 2010, from boston.com/bostonglobe.

McChesney, R. (2005). The emerging struggle for a free press. In R. McChesney & R. Newman (Eds.), *The future of media: Resistance and reform in the 21st century* (pp. 9–20). New York: Seven Stories Press.

McLaren, P. (1999). *Schooling as a ritual performance: Toward a political economy of educational symbols and gestures* (3rd ed.). Lanham, MD: Rowman & Littlefield.

McNamara, M. (June 13, 2006). Teens are wired...and yes, it's ok. *CBS News*. Retrieved February 13, 2011, from cbsnews.com.

McNeil, M. (July 23, 2009). "Race to the Top" guidelines stress use of test data. *Education Week*. Retrieved November 12, 2009, from edweek.org.

McRobbie, A. (1976). Girls and subcultures: An exploration. In S. Hall & T. Jefferson (Eds.), *Resistance through rituals* (pp. 209–222). London: Routledge/Working papers in cultural studies.

McRobbie, A. (1982/1991). The politics of feminist research: Between talk, text and action. In A. McRobbie (Ed.), *Feminism and youth culture* (pp. 118-136). New York: Routledge.

McRobbie, A. (2007). Postfeminism and popular culture: *Bridget Jones* and the new gender regime. In Y. Tasker & D. Negra (Eds.), *Interrogating postfeminism* (pp. 27–39). Durham, NC: Duke University Press.

McRobbie, A. (September 2008). Young women and consumer culture. *Cultural Studies, 22*(5), 531–550.

Menard, L. (June 6, 2011). Live and learn: Why we have college. *The New Yorker*, 74–79.

Mezrich, B. (2009). *The accidental billionaires*. New York: Doubleday.

Miller, C. C. (October 16, 2010). The many faces of you. *The New York Times*. Retrieved February 13, 2011, from nytimes.com.

Miller, C. C. (June 28, 2011). Another try by Google to take on Facebook. *The New York Times*. Retrieved June 29, 2011, from nytimes.com.

Miller, M. (July/August 2003). A new deal for teachers. *The Atlantic*. Retrieved January 12, 2010, from theatlantic.com.

Miron, G., & Applegate, B. (May 2007). Teacher attrition in charter schools. *The Great Lakes Center for Education Research and Practice*. Retrieved February 17, 2010, from greatlakescenter.org

Miron, G., & Nelson, C. (2004). Student achievement in charter schools: What we know and why we know so little. In K. E. Bulkley & P. Wohlstetter (Eds.), *Taking account of charter schools: What's happened and what's next?* (pp. 161–175). New York: Teachers College Press.

Morozov, E. (2011). *The net delusion: How not to liberate the world*. London: Allen Lane.

National Commission on Excellence in Education. (April 1983). *A nation at risk: The imperative for educational reform*.

Newman, R., & Scott, B. (2005). Introduction. In R. McChesney & R. Newman (Eds.), *The future of media: Resistance and reform* (pp. 1–6). New York: Seven Stories Press.

Obama, B. (July 24, 2009). Remarks by the president on education. Retrieved November 12, 2009, from whitehouse.gov.

Otterman, S. (January 19, 2011a). City opens inquiry on grading practices at a top-scoring Bronx school. *The New York Times*. Retrieved January 19, 2011, from nytimes.com.

Otterman, S. (February 7, 2011b). Most New York State students are not college-ready. *The New York Times*. Retrieved February 13, 2011, from nytimes.com.

Parker, N. (February 11, 2011). Revolution in the age of the Internet. *The Los Angeles Times*. Retrieved February 13, 2011, from latimes.com.

Parker-Pope, T. (February 3, 2011). Teenagers, friendships and bad decisions. *The New York Times*. Retrieved February 13, 2011, from nytimes.com.

Paul, P. (October 22, 2010). How to get unfriended on Facebook. *The New York Times*. Retrieved February 13, 2011, from nytimes.com.

Payne, C., & Knowles, T. (Summer 2009). Promise and peril: Charter schools, urban school reform, and the Obama administration. *Harvard Educational Review, 79*(2), 227–239.

Podair, J. E. (2002). *The strike that changed New York: Blacks, whites and the Ocean Hill-Brownsville crisis*. New Haven, CT: Yale University Press.

Projansky, S. (2007). Mass magazine cover girls: Some reflections on postfeminist girls and post-feminism's daughters. In Y. Tasker & D. Negra (Eds.), *Interrogating postfeminism* (pp. 40–72). Durham, NC: Duke University Press.

Putnam, M. (May 30, 2011). Wasting more money. *The New York Times*. Retrieved May 30, 2011, from nytimes.com.

Raice, S. (February 2, 2012). Facebook sets historic IPO. *The Wall Street Journal*. Retrieved February 2, 2012, from wsj.com.

Ravitch, D. (1974/2000). *The great school wars: A history of the New York City public schools*. Baltimore: Johns Hopkins University Press.

Ravitch, D. (1983). *The troubled crusade: American education, 1945–1980*. New York: Basic Books.

Ravitch, D. (2010). *The death and life of the great American school system: How testing and choice are undermining education*. New York: Basic Books.

Rhee, M. (December 6, 2010). What I've learned. *Newsweek*. Retrieved February 13, 2011, from newsweek.com.

Rich, C. (August 2007). Secret life of teens: "Coolest thing ever." *The Washingtonian*. Retrieved February 13, 2011, from washingtonian.com.

Richtel, M. (November 21, 2010). Growing up digital, wired for distraction. *The New York Times*. Retrieved February 13, 2011, from nytimes.com.

Rideout, V. J., Foehr, U. G., & Roberts, D. F. (2010). *Generation M2: Media in the lives of 8- to 18-year-olds*. Menlo Park, CA: Kaiser Family Foundation. Avail: kff.org.

Ripley, A. (November 26, 2008). Rhee tackles classroom challenge. *Time*. Retrieved February 17, 2010, from time.com

Ripley, A. (January/February 2010). What makes a great teacher? *The Atlantic*. Retrieved January 12, 2010, from theatlantic.com.

Roiphe, K. (August 13, 2010). The language of Fakebook. *The New York Times*. Retrieved August 13, 2010, from nytimes.com.

Ross, C., Orr, E. S., Sisic, M., Arseneault, J. M., Simmering, M. G., & Orr, R. R. (2009). Personality and motivations associated with Facebook use. *Computers in Human Behavior, 25*, 578–586.

Rotella, C. (February 2, 2010). Class warrior: Arne Duncan's bid to shake up schools. *The New Yorker*, 24–29.

Rovito, J. (2010). On the "death" of the university. *Culture Machine*. Retrieved December 1, 2010, from culturemachine.net.

Saltman, K. (2002). Junk-king education. *Cultural Studies, 16*(2), 233–258.

Saltman, K. (2005). *The Edison Schools: Corporate schooling and the assault on public education*. New York: Routledge.

Saltman, K. (2007a). *Capitalizing on disaster: Taking and breaking public schools*. Boulder, CO: Paradigm Publishers.

Saltman, K. (2007b). Introduction. In K. J. Saltman (Ed.), *Schooling and the politics of disaster* (pp. 1–21). New York: Routledge.

Saltman, K. (2010). *The gift of education: Public education and venture philanthropy*. New York: Palgrave Macmillan.

Santos, F. (April 8, 2011). Schools' new emissary, from City Hall. *The New York Times*. Retrieved April 8, 2011, from nytimes.com.

Schofield-Clark, L. (2008). The constant contact generation: Exploring teen friendship networks online. In S. R. Mazzarella (Ed.), *Girl wide web: Girls, the Internet and the negotiation of identity* (pp. 203–221). New York: Peter Lang.

Schwandt, T. A. (1998). Constructivist, interpretivist approaches to human inquiry. In N. K. Denzin & Y. S. Lincoln (Eds.), *The landscape of qualitative research: Theories and issues* (pp. 221–259). Thousand Oaks, CA: Sage.

Searls-Giroux, S. (2008–2009). Generation kill: Nietzschean meditations on the university, war, youth, and guns. *Works and Days, 26 & 27*, 473–500. Retrieved June 21, 2011, from worksanddays.net.

Sidorenko, E. (2010). Education, education, education. *Culture Machine*. Retrieved December 1, 2010, from culturemachine.net/index.php/cm/article/view/420/439

Siegel, D. (2007). *Sisterhood, interrupted: From radical women to grrrls gone wild*. New York: Palgrave Macmillan.

Siegel, L. (2008). *Against the machine: Being human in the age of the electronic mob*. New York: Spiegel and Grau.

Smythe, D. (1981). *Dependency road: Communication, capitalism, consciousness and Canada*. Norwood, NJ: Ablex.

Statistics. *Facebook*. Retrieved August 4, 2011, from facebook.com/press/info.php?statistics.

Steinfield, C., Ellison, N. B., & Lampe, C. (2008). Social capital, self-esteem and use of online social network sites: A longitudinal analysis. *Journal of Applied Developmental Psychology, 29*, 434–445.

Tasker, Y., & Negra, D. (2007). Introduction: Feminist politics and postfeminist culture. In Y. Tasker & D. Negra (Eds.), *Interrogating postfeminism* (pp. 1–25). Durham, NC: Duke University Press.

Tavernise, S. (December 1, 2010). A mission to change Baltimore's beaten schools. *The New York Times*. Retrieved December 1, 2010, from nytimes.com.

Taylor, M. C. (2010). *Crisis on campus: A bold plan for reforming our colleges and universities*. New York: Knopf Doubleday.

Thomas, P. (May 30, 2011). Avoiding the poverty issue. *The New York Times*. Retrieved May 30, 2011, from nytimes.com.

Tienken, C. H., & Canton, D. (Fall 2009). National curriculum standards: Let's think it over. *AASA Journal of Scholarship and Practice, 6*(3), 3–9.

Timeline. *Facebook*. Retrieved August 4, 2011, from facebook.com/info.php?timeline.

Tong, S. T., VanDerHeide, B., Langwell, L., & Walther, J. B. (2008). Too much of a good thing? The relationship between number of friends and interpersonal impressions on Facebook. *Journal of Computer-Mediated Communication, 13*, 531–549.

Tough, P. (2008). *Whatever it takes: Geoffrey Canada's quest to change Harlem and America*. Boston: Mariner Books.

Tufekci, Z. (February 2008). Can you see me now? Audience and disclosure regulation in online social network sites. *The Bulletin of Science Technology and Society, 28*(1), 20–36.

Turkle, S. (2011). *Alone together: Why we expect more from technology and less from each other*. New York: Basic Books.

Tyner-Mullings, A. R. (July 31, 2008). *Central Park East Secondary School and the alternative school movement in New York City*. Paper presented at the American Sociological Association Annual Meeting. Retrieved May 23, 2009, from allacademic.com.

United States Department of Education. (March 7, 2009). The American recovery and reinvestment act of 2009: Saving and creating jobs and reforming education. Retrieved November 12, 2009, from ed.gov.

Vargas, J. A. (September 20, 2010). The face of Facebook. *The New Yorker*. Retrieved February 13, 2011, from newyorker.com.

Vargas, J. A. (February 7, 2011). Egypt, the age of disruption and the "me" in media. *The Huffington Post*. Retrieved February 13, 2011, from huffingtonpost.com.

Vargas, L. (2009). *Latina teens, migration and popular culture*. New York: Peter Lang.

Walther, J. B., VanDerHeide, B., Kim, S.-Y., Westerman, D., & Tong, S. T. (2008). The role of friends' appearance and behavior evaluations of individuals on Facebook: Are we known by the company we keep? *Human Communication Research, 34*, 28–49.

Warner, J. (October 3, 2010). Is Rhee's revolution over? When people rebel against education reform. *The New York Times Magazine*, 11–12.

Weber, K (Ed.) (2010). *Waiting for "Superman": How we can save America's failing public schools*. New York: Public Affairs.

Weingarten, R. (2010). Five foundations for student success. In K. Weber (Ed.), *Waiting for "Superman": How we can save America's failing public schools* (pp. 143–161). New York: Public Affairs.

Wells, A. S. (2002). Why public policy fails to live up to the potential of charter school reform: An introduction. In A. S. Wells (Ed.), *Where charter school policy fails: The problem of accountability and equity* (pp. 1–28). New York: Teachers College Press.

Wilder, T., Allgood, W., & Rothstein, R. (November 10, 2008). Narrowing the achievement gap for low-income children: A 19–year life cycle approach. Retrieved June 21, 2011, from epi.org.

Williams, A. (March 9, 2008). A cure for the college-bound blues. *The New York Times*. Retrieved March 9, 2008, from nytimes.com.

Willis, P. (1977). *Learning to labour: How working-class kids get working-class jobs*. New York: Columbia University Press.

Winters, M. (May 30, 2011). Costly, but worth it. *The New York Times*. Retrieved May 30, 2011, from nytimes.com.

Zaslow, E. (2009). *Feminism, Inc.: Coming of age in girl power media culture*. New York: Palgrave Macmillan.

INDEX

CRITICAL ISSUES
FOR LEARNING AND TEACHING
Shirley R. Steinberg & Pepi Leistyna
General Editors

Minding the Media is a book series specifically designed to address the needs of students and teachers in watching, comprehending, and using media. Books in the series use a wide range of educational settings to raise consciousness about media relations and realities and promote critical, creative alternatives to contemporary mainstream practices. *Minding the Media* seeks theoretical, technical, and practitioner perspectives as they relate to critical pedagogy and public education. Authors are invited to contribute volumes of up to 85,000 words to this series. Possible areas of interest as they connect to learning and teaching include:

- critical media literacy
- popular culture
- video games
- animation
- music
- media activism
- democratizing information systems
- using alternative media
- using the Web/internet
- interactive technologies
- blogs
- multi-media in the classroom
- media representations of race, class, gender, sexuality, disability, etc.

- media/communications studies methodologies
- semiotics
- watchdog journalism/investigative journalism
- visual culture: theater, art, photography
- radio, TV, newspapers, zines, film, documentary film, comic books
- public relations
- globalization and the media
- consumption/consumer culture
- advertising
- censorship
- audience reception

For additional information about this series or for the submission of manuscripts, please contact:
Shirley R. Steinberg and Pepi Leistyna,
msgramsci@aol.com | Pepi.Leistyna@umb.edu

To order other books in this series, please contact our Customer Service Department:
(800) 770-LANG (within the U.S.)
(212) 647-7706 (outside the U.S.)
(212) 647-7707 FAX

Or browse online by series:
www.peterlang.com

www.ingramcontent.com/pod-product-compliance
Lightning Source LLC
Chambersburg PA
CBHW070948050326
40689CB00014B/3394